THE DIVORCED MAN'S KITCHEN SURVIVAL GUIDE

A POWERFUL RECIPE TO RECOVER, RENEW AND REBUILD A NEW YOU.

CHRISTOPHER H GILLARD

TEAM CREATIVE
Publishing

THIS IS FOR YOU

For Willow and Lila, *for your unconditional love,*
gentle understanding, unwavering support,
and patience beyond your years,
in the hardest times.

For Susita, *for your deep insights,*
your morning dances, your spirit of adventure,
your fascinating mind, and for seeing me fully,
through your smiling eyes.

And for You, *whoever you are,*
wherever you are on the journey,
you are not alone; this guide is for you.

ABOUT THE AUTHOR

Christopher H Gillard is an Australian who lives in Melbourne, Victoria. He is a qualified chef, professional writer, photographic artist, film maker and a tech entrepreneur with over two decades experience in communications and innovative technology development.

He also happens to be a divorcee who suddenly had to rebuild his life from the ground up in 2019.

Since that time, as one of the Founders, he launched Mindflight7, Australia's biggest and most successful virtual reality careers and education company. He also founded and is Creative Director of Team Creative, an innovation agency specialising in communications and technology development in the areas of artificial intelligence and extended reality (VR, AR, MR) experiences.

Chris's background as a professional chef combined with over 20 years in creative communications and tech innovation provided him with crucial skills and experience needed to successfully navigate the hardest period of his life. It led him to his accidental recipe for renewal and the subsequent creation of this book. He is sharing his story and learnings in the hope of helping others, everywhere.

Please feel free to connect with Chris on Linked In.

Search Linked In: *Chris Gillard Team Creative*

THE DIVORCED MAN'S KITCHEN SURVIVAL GUIDE

"HE WHO CONQUERS HIMSELF IS THE MIGHTIEST WARRIOR."

CONFUCIUS

CHAPTER 1
INTRODUCTION: YOUR NEW SURVIVAL GUIDE

"I WANT A DIVORCE."

THE EX

After 20 years. Her words hit me like a tonne of bricks. Smashed me in the face. Knocked me over. Bloodied my soul. And each time I accidentally recalled them, my heart would race, and I'd find it hard to talk or breathe or think. My mind was swirling. I was mentally punch-drunk. At the time, our two beautiful little girls were five and nine, and it made me deeply sad and sick to the stomach to have to tell them their family life, as they knew it, was over. But that's not all. Unfortunately, as things turned out, and at a horrifyingly fast rate immediately following the separation, I found myself with no job, no savings and *no home*. And every second week I had my girls.

How do you survive this?

Where's the recipe to follow from the moment your separation and divorce is real?

This book describes my journey and what I learned. It also shares the recipe for renewal I accidentally developed on the way. As you read, you will find basic but valuable information about setting up a kitchen, planning meals, cooking regularly for the first time and combining this knowledge and core activity with other positive inputs to create an entirely new and BETTER you.

You'll also find lists of the top common nutritious foods you need in the fridge, freezer and pantry to give you the best chance to renew and support your body and mind. There are also over 30 healthy and tasty recipes that you can make, regardless of your level of cooking experience. And along the way, you will hear my story.

I can show you that no matter what point you are at today, you can come back bigger, better, stronger and wiser. And every new day is an opportunity to improve.

Let me tell you how.

I don't know you, but I'm pretty sure I know the way you feel. I have a very good idea of what you went through or are going through now because I've been there too. Whether you are newly separated, in the process of divorcing, or have recently divorced, I know that awful feeling that you get deep in the gut and in your heart. It's full body pain. It's constant, night and day. It can be debilitating. Whatever happened in your life journey that brought you to this point doesn't matter for this book. What matters now is getting support and gaining insight to help you move forward. This book is only my insight and experience, but I sincerely hope it's positive and valuable for you. I wrote this as much more than a book about food and recipes - I wrote it as a guide to help you get through this moment into a much better place. I hope to help you survive this challenge in your life.

I know that many recently separated or divorced men are unsure of their way around a kitchen. It's a widespread issue that can lead to all sorts of problems. Unless you've been trapped in a mountain cave for the last 40 years, you'll know that the kitchen is a place that welcomes both men and women. However, you might not have the background knowledge of food, nutrition and cooking for confidence in the area. I'm here to tell you that's fine, and now you've got it covered. This book aims to empower men everywhere, just like you, with basic requirements from a kitchen, health and cooking point of view. You will discover cooking skills, nutrition knowledge and self-awareness mixed in with easy, fast, delicious and healthy recipes to build your confidence in the kitchen and yourself.

Before we get into the book, I have some points to make.

The first is the title of the book. While it is for a divorced 'man,' this resource can clearly apply to anyone, any gender. In my life, I welcome all people. This book is the same. Everyone is welcome to read and gain anything from this book. All I hope is that you get something positive out of it. On the same topic, when I mention date night and 'her,' it is simply for illustrative purposes. Whatever pronoun you or your date prefers, the information still stands and you'll be setting yourself up well if you take the pointers, especially the one about smelling nice :)

The second point I want to make is that YOU are NOT your SITUATION. In other words your situation is not YOU. This wisdom was shared with me by my lovely new partner (together five years now!) soon after I met her and it allowed me to move into an entirely new, positive headspace. At the time, I had nothing of value except my car, and I told her exactly that. I was extremely transparent and did not want to waste her time or give her a false impression of me. I asked her what she would want from a man with nothing of value to offer. And she very kindly explained the difference between *me and the situation I was in*. She wasn't concerned about my situation. Why? She saw it would change because she could see ME within it. So please remember that.

Whatever you are dealing with now is just the circumstance; it is not YOU. Do not let the situation trick you into thinking you are one and the same.

The third point I want to make is that while I am all about healthy eating and lifestyle, I also have a strong grasp on reality. This is not a book written by a dietitian or a nutritionist; it is written by a qualified (ex) chef who got separated from his wife, then divorced, and who knew how to cook and maintain a healthy mind and body - and put the knowledge into action. I'm not about low-fat this, salt-reduced that, caffeine-free whatever, or diet drinks. To me, consuming those things is like going sightseeing while wearing a blindfold. I believe the pure form of the item is the best form - just eat or drink less of it! Take comfort from the fact that this book was definitely not written by a "holier than thou" Food Saint! And seriously! Hands up who's never eaten a whole block of rum and raisin chocolate at 2.00 am or sat staring at Netflix at midnight munching on a double cheeseburger with extra ketchup and fries in one hand and unlikely handfuls of dry Froot Loops from the packet in the other, or had moments when a full tub of Ben and Jerry's Triple Caramel Chunk ice cream suddenly evaporated into an empty tub all while you're innocently standing next to the fridge?

After my (let's call them "food mishap" moments), the next day, I'd make sure I drank lots of water and got into some kind of exercise, no matter how pathetic and weak I felt. This was about maintaining the discipline and keeping the routine above all else. If there was no way I could run, I could walk a little. My mind felt better and I felt better because I'd kept to the routine and at least I'd done SOMETHING. The day after that, we're back on track.

I'm sure it's normal for you to have moments when your discipline slips and you find yourself on a junk food and alcohol binge. That's ok! You're only human and I'm not going to tell you otherwise. All I will say is that you must keep your eye on your goals for the medium and long term and make those moments the exception and not the norm. If you're doing the right thing by yourself the majority of the time, you'll be all good.

While we are on about the types of food we eat and why, I want to mention that even though I'm not vegetarian or vegan, I regularly enjoy meals with no meat or animal content whatsoever. There are many parts to the philosophy of veganism and vegetarianism that I do agree with, and I suspect I'm on a journey to remove meat from my diet entirely. It is tough to do this in my household, which includes up to seven people at a time, five of whom are kids!

BEFORE WE BEGIN, A QUICK NOTE ABOUT SOME OF THE FOOD IMAGES IN THIS BOOK.

Take them with a grain of salt, if I may use that term :)

The food images in this book in the kitchen basics and recipe chapters, are illustrations, not photographs, and they're made by Chat GPT AI under my written direction and prompts. I experiment a lot with AI for work in my company and so, for this book, out of professional curiosity more than anything, I decided to make an AI image for each meal and some of the other food images to support the content. You'll know the ones. AI seemed to respond to my written descriptions with a particular art-directional style that would appeal to the sickly sweet eye of a 1950's chocolate box artist. Along with that, it often got the final expression of the food and meal wrong, even after multiple descriptive reviews, by making ingredients too large, too prominent, too voluminous and too structured. Sometimes the background was also a little kooky or downright strange and concerning too, like something from The Twilight Zone.

So when you see the picture of any dish or meal on the following pages, read the image description and probably don't attempt to make a thing that looks exactly like that. Remember that what you are seeing is a picture of the meal and setting I had in my head that I then described to AI, which AI then translated visually into what it had in its...head...or whatever the heck AI has to think with! My point is, if you make a meal from the book, even if it looks like it might be a distant relative to the image, then in all likelihood, you've done well. Good times.

While they are black and white in the print edition (to ensure the printed book is an accessible price to most people), I have left all the pictures AI developed under my direction in the book as an additional point of interest for us. I'd love to hear your thoughts on them!

CHAPTER 2
THE KITCHEN AND LIFE

"LIFE IS NOT ABOUT WAITING FOR THE STORMS TO PASS. IT'S ABOUT LEARNING HOW TO DANCE IN THE RAIN."

VIVIAN GREENE

When you think about it, it's amazing how much of our lives revolve around the kitchen. In most cases, it's the heart of the family home, a central component of life. Families will get together in the kitchen, help each other serve a meal, then connect and eat. The most basic ingredients, put together correctly, can become some of your most memorable meals and moments. It's the same in life, where a blend of simple experiences can become some of your most enduring and special memories. A walk on the beach at sunset with the sand between your toes, a warm, humid sea breeze across your face and a loved one beside you can provide you with profound contentment. Often, the best things aren't complex.

Right now, you are feeling that you have lost all that. You may want to avoid recalling any fond memories because they are much too challenging to look at. That's ok. I know the feeling. That's normal. I can promise you that in the not-too-distant future, you will create new memories that are just as powerful and positive for you. And you can then revisit those times that you can't bear to look at now.

For reasons outlined above, for what it represents, for its symbolic meaning to family, you may not want to enter the kitchen either. I get that - but I need you to do yourself and me a favour.

Just listen.

I will take you back to the kitchen for now because it's vitally important for you. It's essential to your health and your well-being. It's ingredient number one in this recipe. It's important to anyone else you have in your life, including your kids, if you are lucky enough to have them. You may not realise it yet, but getting into the kitchen is vital to your ability to spring back, to be stronger, more experienced and more resilient than ever. I know because I was there, and I worked it out.

If you've never cooked in your life before, it doesn't matter. I could write a five-star fine dining recipe book based on my professional cooking experience in fine restaurants across Australia and include the recipes and techniques of the best French chefs, but that is not what this is. This is a guidebook designed for a time in your life when you need practicality and a solid framework for getting right back up and into it. This is what you have here.

The recipes in this book are not complicated; they don't include wildly exotic ingredients, they don't use terms you won't understand and there's no pretension built into the tone. We aren't about showing off. The food you will make from this book is basic, delicious and healthy. The recipes are about the simplicity, efficiency and nutrition you need for this time in your life.

If you're worried that you'll stuff things up, that you'll get things wrong with a recipe, or that you may not be great in the kitchen, so what? You'll get better. Cooking is a great teacher of life. You will have your trials and errors, the big culinary successes you're proud of, the failures you want to forget. But when you keep going, keep a growth mindset and understand that you are much more capable than you realise, your excitement and feelings of accomplishment will grow. You'll feel great. So keep going. Keep cooking. Cook up your new life. I'm not just trying to inspire you with empty words.

I know all this from experience, and why would I keep it to myself?

As a professionally qualified chef with years of experience in commercial kitchens, I can't tell you how often I've used my experience to navigate difficulties in life and work. I've always got a relevant cooking metaphor, no matter the situation. That's because, for whatever reason, all the trials of cooking seem to reflect the trials of life. Sometimes, we have a recipe to follow and things are easier with that guidance. But other times, we don't.

Sometimes we don't have all the ingredients or are unsure what they are, so we have to improvise and make decisions based on what's in front of us and our best judgement. When you enter the kitchen to cook, remember that it's more than a place to prepare food. It's a place for you to continue the cycle of learning and growing. Right now, you are experiencing the raw ingredients of a new and unfamiliar existence, but when you put them together in the right way, you will nurture a new life full of the flavour, texture and warmth that we all need.

With the kitchen as a central and routine daily location for the next part of your life, let's move on.

CHAPTER 3
WHY I WROTE THIS BOOK

"IT IS NOT THE STRONGEST OF THE SPECIES THAT SURVIVE, NOR THE MOST INTELLIGENT, BUT THE ONE MOST RESPONSIVE TO CHANGE."

CHARLES DARWIN

My mum and dad divorced when I was four. After that, my sister (who is only 13 months older than me) and I stayed with her most of the time. But of course, she had to work. So, from an early age, I grew up getting home from school with my sister well before my mum got home from work. Someone had to help in the kitchen to get things ready for dinner, and I enthusiastically put my hand up. I loved food, so I decided right then that I wanted to be a Chef.

Luckily for me, my mum was an excellent cook, and she noticed my culinary interest very quickly. It was pretty obvious though. In this respect, I was a weird kid with strange tastes for a five-year-old. I was big on coconut rice and avocados. At that age, I ordered Oysters Kilpatrick from the pub, while my sister and best friend Jesse ordered kids' fish and chips. I tried caviar and taramasalata at parties where these things were made to be eaten by the adults in the room. I devoured calves liver with bacon and onion gravy and swilled apple malt vinegar and balsamic from the bottle inside the pantry with the door closed when no one was looking. At one kid's birthday party, the other kids wanted burgers and I requested Lobster Thermidor. I ate stuffed green olives from Greece and Pickled Herring (called Rollmops) from Denmark and I loved them. On an eye-opening weekend when I was only halfway through Primary School, I discovered the amazingness of blue cheese (and other things) on a nudist beach. When she did the grocery shopping, I asked Mum to buy strong, crumbly, mature, vintage Cheddar from the deli. I was into the kick of Tabasco sauce before the age of ten.

Before I hit double digits, I was a two-foot-tall food lover.

So because of these circumstances and my fixation on food, from around the ripe old age of seven, Mum began to teach me everything she knew about cooking. When she was a girl, she was trained by Nannies in French cooking methods, and as a result of this and my vast interest, I learned a lot very fast. I then made all kinds of foods and dinners, including full roasts, complete with roast veggies and apple sauce (for pork roasts). After that, when I went to Dad's place to stay, I began to notice the differences in the food he served and how it was prepared. It was always a lucky dip of delicious recipes and dishes from Mum on one hand and consistent Frozen Fish Fingers and Baked Beans from Dad on the other. Don't get me wrong - my Dad was and is an amazing, caring, fun Dad, and I still genuinely love Fish Fingers and Baked Beans. I've never suffered from "foodie pretension" (which I consider ridiculous because food is a basic requirement of life, not a status symbol). Still, the differences in their meal offerings were stark.

Dad did what he could with food, and I loved it, but what if he had known how to do even more?

From that early age, I grew up with a vow that I would never get divorced. I wanted a family that I could call my own and I wanted kids who would never experience the pain of divorce that I did. I vowed that my kids would never experience the sorrow of a shattered family, of having parents who split forever.

But that was not how my story was written. In late June 2019, after 20 years and during a particularly hard financial period, my wife left me.

I want a divorce.

What was I supposed to do?

First I had to get back up. I knew I just had to get off the floor. So I did. It was hard, but I got up. I looked around. I hadn't lost everything. I still had my amazing girls. That was more than enough to get me back in the ring. I still had my cooking skills too. And I hadn't lost the tenacity, resilience, forced creativity and ridiculous hopefulness that comes from years of self-inflicted punishment as an entrepreneur in a startup environment.

My ability to move on from that point was accelerated and assisted by my decision to adapt to circumstances quickly and look after my mental and physical health and that of my daughters, with good food and proper meals.

Image: While I was pet-sitting in 2019, among many other meals, I made these vegetable fritters with balsamic glaze and goat's cheese. They were awesome, thank you.

The kitchen was ground zero; the epicentre of my personal relaunch and the start of my new life.

I am unsure how my story would have unfolded if I had not had the skills to cook healthy, delicious meals with minimal resources. You probably wouldn't be hearing this. What could I say? My knowledge at that time was a superpower for me, and now it is time for me to share some of what I experienced with you and others who might benefit.

I genuinely hope that you and newly separated and divorced men everywhere will be strengthened, inspired and renewed by this book. I know you can get back on your feet and go forward in life in confidence and in health and along the way, find happiness again. You do it by maximising the good inputs into your body and your new life and removing the bad ones. You do it by creating a positive new routine to go along with your new reality. You change the environment and the daily things you see, to let your brain know things are new and different.

I know these things because that's my story.

I discovered that separation and divorce are the end of something while also being the start of another thing. And believe me, it can be a better thing, a positive thing.

For you, my reader, I promise you, and I will repeat it for clarity - you can find true happiness again. I sincerely hope this book helps you succeed in that.

CHAPTER 4
GET YOUR PERSONAL BASICS SORTED

"LIFE IS A JOURNEY THAT MUST BE TRAVELLED NO MATTER HOW BAD THE ROADS AND ACCOMMODATIONS."

OLIVER GOLDSMITH

There were many challenges I experienced having to immediately adjust to life after separation and then divorce, and I am sure you are tackling similar issues.

I was dealing with a lot, but my biggest problem was suddenly not having a home or any place to live.

I always walk to think. The process activates alpha wave rhythms in your brain, you get relaxed and your capacity for creativity increases. So contemplating my major problem, I was (somewhat randomly) wandering the streets considering the expense of a tent when a scruffy little dog with no collar, long brown hair, bright eyes, a big smile and a metronome tail suddenly appeared right in my path. I have no idea where he came from. I looked down at him carefully. He seemed more like a quick pencil sketch of a dog rather than a real one, but there he was. I wondered if he was homeless too. His little brown eyes kept looking up at me. As we continued to meet each other's gaze, I know it sounds weird, but it was as if he was communicating with me. It was uncanny. And while we did this, and I crouched down and ruffled his coat, I wondered where he lived. Where was HIS home? And boom! That's when he gave me the idea. I stood up abruptly as I realised this could be a real solution. And as I did, he just bolted, right down the footpath and into a little park with some swings. And I never saw him again.

Thanks to Sketch (that's his proper name in my opinion), I joined a pet-sitting website and it saved me and the girls. I was still homeless, but I had found a solution that gave me places I could stay where I didn't have to pay rent or regular household bills. In return for carefully looking after their home and pets, my girls and I were able to temporarily reside in the homes of others while they were away. It was a great short-term solution, and I will be eternally grateful Sketch's telepathic pawers (deliberate mis-spelling) and for the people, their homes, their pets and the online platform that gave me this bridging security at this very uncertain time in my life.

Image: I used to take pictures of people's pets to send to them while they were away. This chilled guy is one of them.

I learned a few things from my pet-sitting experience that I can pass on. The first is that there are total strangers willing to be very kind to you in your situation. This attitude I encountered in strangers contrasted starkly against the actions and reactions of those I knew well. I did not have anyone from my side of the family in the city where we lived. My freshly "ex" wife had her whole family 15 minutes away, so she had plenty of immediate support, which I am happy about. You would think I might have expected the same after 20 years of knowing these people and sharing many beautiful family moments, but unfortunately, from that end, there was total radio silence and they acted as an "ex" family.

How lovely.

This silence from my ex's family made no sense to me. I was not abusive. I was not unkind. I was not negative. I was not an absent father. I was not lazy, I was not an alcoholic or drug taker and I did not cheat on my wife. In fact, I was the exact opposite of all these things. My parents were both in other states, thousands of kilometres away, so while they were wonderfully supportive on the phone as the two people who knew me best, I was astounded that other people who I thought of as family and who also knew me pretty bloody well - would not so much as even give me a call. It shook me. It did not make sense. I was confused. Why? Add to this the fact that the friends we shared were suddenly non-existent too. That has been hard for me to forget.

I did not know then why our couple friends were not checking up on me or being supportive. My personal friendship group at that time was pretty small and consisted mainly of our neighbours, some of whom had become good friends over the years, or at least I thought they were. I was entirely focused on the family and did not feel the need to have lots of other friends as I was very busy with work and felt I had everything I needed. But even these people were standoffish. I didn't know why at the time. I would bet that you have had the same or a similar experience.

I have since learned that a marriage breakup often confronts friends. Sometimes, it is because they are worried about their own marriage. Sometimes, they support the one who seems most in need - and it's often not the man. Other times, it is because they are just not therapists and do not know how to help you even if they want to. And then, at other times, they may have been given false, misleading, or implied information about the breakup and its alleged causes that make them avoid you or even entirely write you off. All these are common factors, and any of them might play into the reality that you are probably not receiving the level of support from friends and family you might reasonably expect. I'm just here to tell you it's normal and usually, with friends, it is not personal. Dealing with these kinds of things is hard for everyone, so people often try to avoid getting involved. When you are in the middle of this situation and it's new, you can find yourself becoming sad and then angry at all those who don't have your back, but should.

You know what? Let that go. It is a useless waste of your energy.

Instead, put your negative energy into positive physical expression in exercise.

Run it off.

Work it out.

Improve yourself.

Get better.

Feed your body well.

Come back stronger.

Right now, focus on you, not others, unless they're your kids. And if you have kids, then it's even more important to be the best version of yourself.

When I registered on the pet-sitting site, it was a real financial risk because although it was not a major expense in my normal life, paying an annual fee for site registration was a big deal when all I had was a few hundred dollars my dad loaned me to live on. What if no one wants me? Where will I stay then? I needed to create a profile, but I was not ready to admit I was a separated man who had lost everything except his two gorgeous daughters. I felt like I was a failure and I was still perplexed about the lack of contact from friends and my ex-wife's side of the family.

I put up the best photo of myself I could find for the profile and a couple of super cute pictures of my daughters. Then I made up a wonderfully wholesome story about my desire to give my little girls some offbeat educational adventure with animals and pets while exploring different parts of the city and discovering how other people live.

Image: I had to pick a photo of myself for the pet-sitting site profile that would give people confidence that I was not a serial killer who was going to secretly copy the front door key, then insert himself into their lives, stalk the family relentlessly before disappearing and hiding in the roof for two weeks and then cunningly burning down the house while also looking like the hero who was trying to put it out. Given that serial killers are often charming and good-looking it was tough.

As if anyone believed that rubbish. Of course, everyone knew it was a cover story. But they kindly played along. Well, all except for the first lady whose house and Jack Russel puppy (Max) we looked after. She was very kind and very German as well. She asked me to come and see her so we could chat and she could get a sense of me before potentially accepting me as the pet sitter.

When I arrived, I had my fingers crossed and my carefree modern hippy story worked out. She got me inside, sat me on the couch and immediately said in the straightforward way that only the Germans can,

> *"So, when did you get divorced?"*

When I could speak again, I told her the truth, she nodded, then immediately shoved me out the door before systematically parading me to numerous single women in the same apartment block. And she told me I had the job. (I was like, hang on, what job exactly?)

That was the start of my first three weeks of pet-sitting.

Image: The smaller one is Max, the first dog I looked after when I was pet-sitting.

Image: Max was a very photogenic subject.

I realise now that everyone who allowed me to help them in their homes and look after their pets knew they were giving us a home we needed. They all showed much more empathy, care and compassion for me and my daughters than people I'd known for years.

I stayed in some beautiful homes when I was pet-sitting. I never felt the negative emotions of jealousy or envy for what others had. Instead, I felt the benefits of what they had given me. Pet-sitting gave me not just a roof and beds but long moments of silence, lots of space, new, interesting environments, and unconditional love from big dogs, small dogs, cats, kittens, chickens, a Cockatiel, an Alpaca, a donkey and a little turtle with a weird, unfortunate skin issue.

Through pet-sitting I was given the opportunity to clear my mind and think. It was at times lonely, and at other times, the stillness and solitude were welcome as they allowed for reflection, meditation, refocus and peace. I could see many other people's lives from the inside and dwell deeply upon them. In seeing other lives, I realised I could create any life I wanted at any moment I wanted. I was reminded that every second represents infinite possibilities.

I remembered a moment when I was about 11 years old.

I was in the central Queensland gem-fields with my dad and it was the mid-eighties. The hair was bad. The music was great. Men at Work, AC/DC and INXS were huge. Add any of their songs to this scene. It was a rough and rugged environment, the epitome of pure Australian outback. In my kid's brain, half the dudes we met out there were either ex-prisoners or should have been. We were on the hunt for sapphires; an amazing, almost magical adventure for me. We sought the hidden sparkles in the earth during the day while the sky revealed its own celestial jewels and mystery at night. And one of those nights, as I looked up in total awe, I started trying to count the stars in a tiny patch of sky above me. I quickly gave up, but the process gave me a jolting realisation about the world and our universe. Because, as I was counting the stars, I decided to change their name to 'possibilities.'

Each star was now known to me as a *possibility*.

Trying to count them was immediately helpful in my partial understanding of the fact that they were infinite. So I stood there, alone at night, looking up in the Australian outback with my mouth wide open, seeing and suddenly grasping the reality of infinite possibilities right above me. And they are there every night, above all of us. That is something I have never forgotten, and it will be helpful for you to remember it right now, too. The cosmic vastness of the universe is a mirror to our own potential.

Image: This is how AI visualised my memory of my moment in the gem-fields when I was a kid. Look up and out and see limitless possibilities on any night. Do it tonight. Understand that there are no boundaries to what is possible and that this is a Universal Truth.

As a pet-sitter, you normally stay at a place between two days and a week, maybe two weeks if you're lucky. It is quite random and stressful if it is your only housing option, yet it never overwhelmed me. Most of the time, I was online looking for the next place and trying to make the new location work for getting my girls to school and back without driving for hours. It was truly a logistical nightmare and a major ongoing operation. Sometimes, inevitably, I had gap days with no place to stay, but thankfully, through luck or design, those were times I did not have the girls. Perhaps the lowest point for me was one night in late October 2019. I did not have any place to stay that night. I went somewhere I did not want to go.

I arrived under the cover of darkness. Our old family home was locked up, entirely emptied of all things, with water, gas and electricity turned off. I had the house key and a rolled mattress. I took it from the car.

With a deep feeling of dread, I slowly opened the front door and stared down the long hallway. It was inky black. A sudden wave of emotions hit me, another familiar, powerful body slam that doubled me over in pain. Life and love had been drained from every inch of the house and its very heart had been ripped from the building. As I made myself recover and move forward, each footstep echoed loudly on the wooden floor. It was a cruel reminder of the emptiness surrounding me; nothing left to embrace the sounds and smooth their sharp edges.

I didn't know where to stay. Each room was loaded and triggering. I finally decided to stay in the room that had been the nursery. When I unrolled and sat on the mattress, the silence of a once loud, happy, fun home amplified my loneliness to 11 on a scale of 10. I broke through the darkness with the single, pitiful beam of my phone flashlight and looked around at nothing. I turned it off, lay down and tried to sleep. I was desperate to push time forward to a new day. I could not. For now, I had to lie there and confront the ghosts in a house that had once been a home. Outside, other ghosts wandered the streets.

It was October 31st. Halloween.

You might have your own Halloween moment. Whatever that might be, remember it is just a moment. You are not a static being and you can change your situation. Remember your strength. When everything seems out of control, remember that getting back up and moving forward is one thing you can control. Being successful in any small way or any big way, is something you can control.

I continued my journey the next day, off to the next place.

CHAPTER 5
THE ROAD TO SOMEWHERE

"DO NOT GO WHERE THE PATH MAY LEAD, GO INSTEAD WHERE THERE IS NO PATH AND LEAVE A TRAIL."

RALPH WALDO EMERSON

As a pet-sitter, I found myself driving more than I had ever driven in my life. I was always on a road to somewhere. But I never got the feeling it was a road *to nowhere*. I just was not aware of where it would take me. I began to see my driving as the constant physical expression of my deeper spiritual journey. Despite the massive uncertainty of my existence this travelling represented, I was strangely calm. I treated the whole thing like an observer who was supposed to travel to find answers if I looked for them.

So that's what I did.

One thing I do, and love, is landscape photography. There was a moment a couple of months after the separation when I had a gap period - no place to stay - and about $23 in my account. It was then, almost unbelievably - at the perfect moment really, that I won a job to develop a commissioned landscape art piece. And with that came an immediate bank deposit which for me, was significant.

As a photographic artist, in 2008, I invented a method of deconstructing my Australian landscape photography, then printing each colour element of the image on layered glass panels to create large-format three-dimensional (3D) landscape artworks.

Image: This is 'Bowser' a 3D layered glass image from my Fragile Landscapes art series.

This art series is called 'Fragile Landscapes' and explores environmental and sustainability themes. My work is produced as standalone glass art pieces and integrated into architecture.

The job I won required me to be in the Victorian goldfields region for several weeks, wandering the land and capturing a wide variety of landscape images before my client would pick one to integrate into their renovated property in an artistic collaboration between me, the architect and builder. The accommodation in the area was paid for, as well as a daily allowance for food and drink. It was an incredibly lucky break. Given my mental state at the time, I was particularly concerned that I would be blind to the beauty of the world, that I was too internally depleted, that my artistic mojo was non-existent and that any new images I tried to create would be stillborn; dead and buried from the start. But I was given the opportunity and the job, and I was determined to do it extremely well for my client, my girls and myself.

Image: This is another one from the Fragile Landscapes art series of 3D layered glass images. It's called 'Clouds Gather'.

So began a period of weeks in the goldfields when I woke up before sunrise every day to head out to attempt to capture something special. I'd do that for an hour or two, until just after first light, then I'd go home to eat breakfast. Mid-morning to mid-afternoon, I then explored all the nooks and crannies of the region. I drove down the empty country roads, which turned into the little country lanes and then onto long dusty tracks and then onto animal pathways through the fields until I saw or felt whatever I was looking for. I journeyed each day with no idea where I would end up. Most of the time, I'd need to stop and travel those animal paths; walk among the hills, through the fields, beside the creek, or up the mountain. The whole time, I rarely saw another person, which, over the days, seemed more and more unlikely and unnatural but which also gave the whole experience a gradually building spiritual aura as if I had been taken from earth and presented with my own universe to wander about in. Or maybe I was Player 1 in a giant sim? Or was I just exploring the inside of my own mind?

My daily routine might have looked like an aimless process to a casual observer, but I knew it wasn't; this is how I discovered inspiration. You need to get to know your subject when photographing a person for a portrait. It's the same with the land. You get to know it first and never know what you'll find until you come across it. Sometimes even when you take the shot, you don't know what you've found. After my reconnaissance trips, I'd go home in the afternoon, eat some lunch and then head out to one of the special places I'd discovered earlier to photograph it in its best light: at sunset and in the twilight. I would do the same thing the next morning. And the process would repeat.

Image: This is ''Beehive Mine' one of the images I created as part of my goldfields photographic art job.

This Fragile Landscapes loop was a month-long meditation, an entirely peaceful but disciplined artistic routine that I now realise, allowed me to convert my negative emotions into a positive result. It forced me to be creative and reveal emotional expression at a key moment in my life. I had inadvertently found a way to expel my feelings positively through a creative process, but I had no idea of the quality of what I was creating. Every day, I could see my new pictures before me, but I really didn't know if they were good, bad or just embarrassing.

Image: This is ''Lake Ruins 1' It's one of about 30 final images I selected to show to my client.

While it was a sorrowful moment in my life, I was never alone when I was out in the open. The phrase "I was existing with nature" does not come close to describing the power of what happened and the feelings I had. Nature was more than kind to me; she was a perfect therapist. When people say that nature heals, it's true. If you're recently separated, I hope you can soon spend some time in therapy with nature and create something too, because I know the process works. It doesn't matter what you do, just get out there and create. It might sound like Hippy mumbo jumbo to you but it really helps you change your state of mind. And when you look up at night, it helps you see those stars.

Somehow, I captured some of my most compelling images in that period. It was stunning to hear my clients, who were totally unaware of my situation, describe my photos as romantic, wistful, nostalgic, beautiful, poetic...I'd say there's a whole psychology book in them.

Image: This is called ''Lone Tree and Field'. (See what I mean by a psychology book?).

Image: This is another one: ''Moolort Sunset Field'.

CHAPTER 6
YOU CAN STAND THE HEAT

"WE CANNOT BECOME WHAT WE WANT BY REMAINING WHAT WE ARE."

MAX DE PREE

As I moved around, stayed in different places and met different animals (and their people), I also began to see various kitchens and pantries and the insides of fridges, the real belly of the home. Often, the people would have food and drinks in the fridge that they encouraged me and the girls to consume, or they would leave all kinds of edible things and various liquids as parting gifts to make me feel welcome which was a huge bonus and something I had not expected or anticipated. The whole thing really was a great expression of generosity of spirit and a true blessing for us, but what was interesting to me, in a professional sense, was the situation allowed me to audit a number of diverse kitchen environments and work out the most valuable and necessary kitchen ingredients and appliances. Within my context of having essentially nothing, I was developing a list of foods, utensils and appliances that were most important for this time in my life. This is some of the knowledge I'm sharing with you now. These are some of the more practical answers.

Another learning I took from pet-sitting was the importance of daily discipline, and a component of that was keeping each person's home clean. To begin with, because I needed great profile reviews from each homeowner, I ensured their home was cleaner when they got back than when they left. While they were still away, I also sent them portrait pictures of their pets.

Who's not going to love that?

Image: I wasn't sure if the cat loved me or hated me.

Image: This dog definitely loved me and his toy.

Image: There were seven more, just like this one.

Their high rating reviews gave confidence to the next person who would get me to look after their pet and home. Every day, I followed a cleaning process, and the discipline of keeping things clean became a habit I actually enjoyed. Without being obsessive, I looked forward to my cleaning work. It was very satisfying to stay in a pristine, uncluttered environment and then, when homeowners arrived back, to receive positive feedback from grateful people when I really needed it. Most interestingly, the cleanliness of my environment helped me focus, think clearly and stay positive. I have now discovered that this is because the environment you're in has a strong effect on the mind that can be negative or positive. A dirty, cluttered environment can promote anxiety and will send an unconscious message to the brain that you're disorganised and not in control. You do not want to be negatively reinforcing your situation like this. While the discipline of keeping things clean might be difficult for you to maintain initially, make sure you keep it up. When you clean, you are telling your brain through the visual cortex that *you are in control and dealing with things,* which is an essential message for your subconscious and conscious brain now. If I kept it up, I found that most cleaning tasks were less than five minutes each and a tidy home was easy. So imagine yourself making daily cleaning a habit. It feels good, and you will feel good.

My income from my artwork helped to pay the ongoing basic bills of food and petrol, but things were extremely tight, and I was not in the mood to spend any more than I needed to. Because of this, when it came to food, I used my experience and began shopping like a chef. I made focused purchases, planned meals and menus, went for the specials, made leftovers into new meals and wasted nothing. I shopped at the cheapest supermarket, where, ironically, I commonly found the highest quality and best value foods.

Image: This is beef with guacamole, and I made it in a stranger's home. Yes, it was delicious, thanks for asking.

When purchasing ingredients for any recipe in this book, *but only when you can really afford it*, I suggest you buy organic foods, biodynamic foods, hormone-free and free-range meats and other products that are entirely natural and exclude pesticides, insecticides and all the poisonous extras corporate psychopaths like to add to plants and animals that can massively damage our own bodies and the earth. It is ridiculous and insane to ingest foods that include chemical cocktails that are proven to cause cancer and kill other sentient beings on our planet. Still, often, we do not have a choice and most of the time it's for economic reasons. It is one of the most unfair aspects of our existence as a species that the most natural foods, full of the most goodness that nature can provide, are also the most expensive and unattainable for the majority of household budgets and people.

20 REGULAR USE KITCHEN UTENSILS AND APPLIANCES

Contrary to what all the food shows might communicate, you don't need every device under the sun to cook well. However, there are a few items you need in the kitchen to operate confidently and create some variety in what you make. This chapter lists the ideal and essential tools, utensils and appliances your kitchen should have to give you flexibility in what you can do without going over the top.

Based on my experience, these are the most useful basic kitchen utensils and appliances you need to create a variety of nutritious foods you require to fuel yourself properly and anyone else you are looking after. You'll get a functional, versatile and flexible kitchen while you also create a revised daily routine, operate in a new environment and include additional positive inputs in your life.

- **Chef's knife:** This one's big and is used for chopping, dicing and mincing.
- **Paring knife**: These are little knives, often with curved blades, used for peeling and slicing smaller fruits and vegetables.
- **Cutting board:** Of course you need this. A must-have for safe and efficient chopping. Ensure it is secure on the bench too, or you will cut yourself.
- **Mixing bowls:** You need them and the stainless steel ones are the best. Get them in various sizes for mixing and preparing ingredients.
- **Whisk**: You will use this for mixing batters, sauces and dressings.
- **Wooden spoon:** Same reason your mum had one - for dealing with bad children, as well as their secondary use for stirring and mixing, especially in non-stick pans.
- **Spatula:** For when you flip and scrape stuff.
- **Tongs:** Get two or three of these in a couple of sizes and not the flimsy crap. Use for flipping and turning foods, especially when frying or grilling.
- **Peeler**: Does what it says. For fruits and vegetables.
- **Can opener:** I really don't need to explain this, do I?

- **Colander:** A bowl with small holes. For draining pasta and washing vegetables.
- **Blender:** You need this for smoothies, soups and sauces.
- **Food processor:** For now, you could probably take it or leave it, but if you can get one, it is great for chopping, slicing, and mixing large quantities of food.
- **Microwave:** Goes without saying - but it's not for cooking. It's for quick reheating or defrosting.
- **Toaster or toaster oven:** Underrated. Very helpful.
- **Electric kettle:** I'm not explaining this either.
- **Pan or frying pan:** A heavy-based one is the best. Cast iron is even better. These are very important; you will often use yours for frying, sautéing and searing.
- **Saucepan:** Get a few sizes. These are for boiling, simmering, poaching, making soups and sauces - all kinds of stuff.
- **Oven trays:** The heavier and deeper ones are better as they don't burn your food at the base, are more adaptable to different foods and can contain liquids. These are necessary for any baking, roasting and slow cooking.
- **Music:** Every commercial kitchen I have ever worked in has the music going. It's amazing what it does to the vibe, the energy levels and your creative capacity. So you need some kind of music going when you cook. Music will make cooking fun, define your new routine and positively regulate your emotions. I use a portable Bluetooth speaker called a Boom, but anything you can play music on will work. It even helps with the washing up!

The music, along with all these utensils and appliances in your kitchen, means that you can work with various cooking methods and prepare a wide variety of dishes while developing a soundtrack to your new culinary routine. Now you've got the operational basics you need.

Wait, where's the bottle opener?

I'm guessing you might feel like a drink at this time in your life. I am sure that's normal and I will not tell you not to. I drank after separation. I expected to drown my sorrows constantly. But for some reason, I didn't do that. However, I wouldn't tell you not to drink excessively because who am I to judge? And I'm not a professional who can give an opinion like that. You already know it's bad. If drinking is a struggle for you, then all I'd say is, please see a health professional ASAP, and I am sure you will feel infinitely better for having taken that action.

Image: This AI image of kitchen utensils shows that AI gets weirdly excited about whisks.

USING KNIVES

Since you're going to cook, you'll be using knives. Because different knives serve various purposes, getting to know their uses is a good way to enhance the quality of your meal preparation and the outcomes of your cooking.

The basic knives used by chefs

Chef's Knife: My second most used knife. This versatile knife has a blade about 8 to 10 inches long. It's perfect for slicing, dicing and chopping all kinds of things. The slightly curved edge also makes it perfect for mincing things finely, like herbs (by rocking the knife back and forth).

Paring Knife: With a short blade (about 3-4 inches), this knife is excellent for peeling fruits and vegetables, trimming and other tasks requiring precision. Be very careful with this one. Go slow.

Serrated or Bread Knife: This one is easily recognisable by its saw-like edge. It is perfect for slicing bread or tomatoes without crushing them or slicing the thick skin off a pineapple.

Utility Knife: I use this most often. Larger than a paring knife but smaller than a chef's knife, the utility knife is good for general tasks, like slicing meat and cheese.

USING YOUR KNIVES SAFELY

This book is not a knife training guide. It is not intended to teach you knife skills and handling, which you will have to learn elsewhere under professional supervision, but I think it is valuable for you to understand how to be safe with knives.

Proper Cutting Board Stability: This is very important. Make sure you do it. When I went to chef school, the VERY FIRST LESSON in the teaching kitchen was about keeping your cutting board stable to prevent injury. To do this, first, make sure your cutting board is entirely flat (some old ones curve a bit). Now, place your cutting board over a damp towel or kitchen paper to prevent it from moving. A stable surface makes it easier and much safer to cut.

Keep Fingers Curled Away: Always curl your fingers inward when holding food. This technique is known as the 'claw grip,' and it protects your fingertips. Let the knuckles, rather than the fingertips, guide the knife.

Angle the Blade Away From Fingers: Ensure the blade is always angled away from your fingers. This minimises the risk of accidental cuts. Just doing this has saved me and my digits multiple times.

Use a Sharp Knife: This is really important. A sharp knife is much safer than a blunt one because it requires less force to cut through ingredients. Less force means you have more control, reducing the chance of the knife slipping. Regularly sharpen your knives to maintain their efficiency. You can watch videos online about this.

Wear strong shoes: Always be mindful of your fingers *and your toes*. Remember that knives get dropped accidentally so when you are cooking, wear strong shoes and keep other people's feet away from the immediate food prep area, especially kids.

Knife Handling: You can learn more about this via other resources but as a quick description: grip the handle of the chef's knife with your dominant hand, placing your thumb on one side of the blade and your index finger on the opposite side, slightly curled around the handle for control. This type of grip gives you better command of the knife and precision.

Cutting Motion: For most cutting tasks, use a fluid rocking motion. Start with the knife tip on the cutting board, then push down and forward, allowing the blade to rock through the food. This motion is efficient for chopping herbs or vegetables. Go slow. Get the rhythm going.

Cleaning Knives: NEVER put sharp knives into soapy water or you risk major injury to yourself or someone else. Wash knives by hand instead of in the dishwasher to maintain their edges. Dry them immediately to prevent rust and then put them away safely in a knife block away from children or into a similar safe environment.

Practising Knife Skills: Practice is key to developing better skill at anything and using knives is just the same. I mentioned this before and I'll state it again. Start slow. And then go slow. I strongly suggest you watch a few videos online about using knives safely and keeping them sharp. In the kitchen, pay attention to accuracy and safety, not speed. Staying careful, you will improve over time. Do not rush your knife use!

Image: This AI image of a huge kitchen with an assortment of knives includes two ovens, two island benches and wild amounts of utensils. Why?

CHAPTER 7
THE SECOND ARROW

"WHAT DOES NOT KILL US MAKES US STRONGER."

FRIEDRICH NIETZSCHE

I have provided this quote because I want to highlight my disagreement with it. I think this:

> What does not kill us, does not kill us. But it is we, that decide to make ourselves stronger.

You and I both know a marriage breakup or separation is hugely stressful and traumatic. All of us can experience not only mental anguish but we will also see physical manifestations of our stress. For me, this included disrupted sleep, reduced appetite and lower energy. You might have the same symptoms, as well as increased blood pressure, weakened immune function, or other physical issues. Whatever way your situation might be affecting you physically, right now, I can tell you with 100% certainty that, apart from professional help, focusing on your diet and exercise is the most crucial thing you can do in this period.

When you do that, then this is you making you stronger.

I know very well that the combination of a balanced diet and regular exercise creates a synergy that can significantly mitigate the effects of stress because I proved it for myself in the separation and divorce period of my life. Focusing on a nutritious diet gave me the energy and nutrients necessary for my planned exercise. At the same time, my physical activity, in turn, improved the quality of my sleep and reduced my cravings for unhealthy foods. This positive feedback cycle promoted and reinforced my physical and mental well-being and improved my confidence and interactions with others.

The recipe was simple: mix a healthy diet with regular exercise to relieve stress and anxiety and get stronger in every way.

I am a living example that when you are navigating the stress of a marriage breakup or separation, prioritising diet and exercise is not just about maintaining physical health; it's about creating a foundation for emotional resilience and renewal which leads to a new identity. By focusing on nutrition and physical activity, as I did, you can navigate the challenges of this life transition with greater strength, stability, and optimism, laying the groundwork for a healthier future and a brand new you.

When my wife left me, I had enough background knowledge of the link between exercise and diet to mental health and my overall functioning to formulate a recipe for stabilising my situation and creating a pathway to a better place. While I was under heavy emotional stress and taking it day by day, I still had a forward-thinking attitude and a plan for where I wanted to get to. And my positive attitude and planning mindset, helped me avoid the full force of the 'Second Arrow'.

The Second Arrow is a Buddhist concept I was unaware of at the time, that represents the <u>self-inflicted pain</u> of your negative thoughts and emotions. This arrow comes after the First Arrow; the unavoidable suffering in life. Like you, I felt the full, devastating force of the First Arrow when my wife left me, but I managed to avoid major damage from the Second Arrow. While I was certainly grappling with the negative force of the Second Arrow, as it tried to hit me in the same spot as the first, I was able to divert it into a positive place. This is because, unlike the first, I was IN CONTROL of the Second Arrow. The control allowed me to talk to my children honestly and authentically about the separation. I told them very early on, that their mother deserved to be happy, I wanted her to be happy, and that these things can happen in life. I told them it was ok and they still had both of us to love them. While I was totally confused at how this had happened, I did not want my children to feel the compounded pain of their own Second Arrow through my own weakness. Meanwhile, I sweated out my anger, pain, confusion, anxiety and self-pity and other unhelpful feelings in regular exercise and being kind to myself like I would be to a friend. In this way, I was able to maintain a focus on compassion, acceptance and letting go. I did not want to make a bad situation worse.

I do not follow Buddhism or any other religion, but I avoided the negative impact of the Second Arrow simply because I decided to be accepting of what had happened. Why try to hold onto a person who isn't happy in the relationship? If anything, this is just a clear sign that she is not for me and I am not for her. And that's ok.

You not only have this moment in your life as a foundation for both physical and emotional healing and renewal, you also have a crossroads moment to create an entirely new you.

So take advantage of it right now.

CHAPTER 8
FUELING YOUR BODY AND MIND

"LET FOOD BE THY MEDICINE AND MEDICINE BE THY FOOD."

HIPPOCRATES

When going through major stress, you need high-quality, nutrient-rich foods more than you would in a normal period. The foods I have outlined in this book and its recipes are included for this reason. They are high in vitamins, minerals and antioxidants that can help combat the physiological effects of your stress by boosting the immune system and reducing inflammation.

A diet rich in vegetables, fruits, whole grains, lean proteins and healthy fats provides the essential nutrients you need now for optimal mental health and brain functioning. Here's what's good about them.

- **Omega-3 Fatty Acids**: Found in fish like salmon, mackerel, and sardines, as well as in flaxseeds and walnuts, omega-3s can reduce inflammation and have been linked to lower levels of depression.
- **Whole Grains**: Foods like whole wheat pasta, brown rice, and oatmeal are rich in complex carbohydrates, which help maintain levels of serotonin, a brain neurotransmitter that promotes well-being.
- **Leafy Greens and Vegetables**: Spinach, kale, and broccoli (detailed later) are packed with vitamins and minerals, including B vitamins, which are vital for energy production and the management of stress in the body.

- **Lean Protein:** Things like chicken, turkey, beans, and lentils provide amino acids necessary for neurotransmitter function, supporting mood and cognitive function during stressful times.
- **Probiotics:** Foods rich in probiotics, such as yoghurt, kefir and fermented vegetables, all support gut health which is closely linked to mood and mental health due to the fascinating gut-brain axis.

THE ROLE OF EXERCISE IN THE NEW YOU

I know firsthand that exercise is a powerful stress reliever. In the immediate aftermath of my separation, I added a run to my daily routine. Of course, it wasn't a daily marathon and I built up the distance over time, but it had multiple significant positive effects from the start. One of the most interesting outcomes was that a run ADDED to my energy levels and REDUCED my tiredness. It is counterintuitive, but when you expend energy with exercise, you can often receive an energy boost afterward. How cool is that? For me, this also came with renewed mental clarity and the ability to focus and get work done. Running is very meditative when you get into the rhythm and it can help you sort problems in your mind, often with relative ease. So inside, I was pleased with myself after every run. I felt stronger and better about my body and more excited to do it again tomorrow. So, in this way, I began to build up a positive feedback loop. The more I exercised, the more I saw benefits, the better I felt, and the more motivated I became. I felt like I was taking control of my situation and it felt good.

All this from the FIRST run onwards. Imagine going on that first run. You can do this too.

Along with running, I did two more strength building exercises every day that rounded out the workout. I didn't need any equipment either. They were simple push-ups and sit-ups. I built up the reps from 30 a day to 300 a day of each (30 x 10 sets).

I am not a personal trainer, and I don't know what exercise routine is most appropriate for you, but I'm sure you understand. Whatever exercise you choose to do and at any level is an important part of the recipe for the new you.

Whatever exercise might be right for you, it will help to release built-up tension and produce endorphins, which are chemicals in the brain that act as natural painkillers and mood elevators.

As you will find out, regular physical activity can improve your sleep, enhance your self-esteem and provide a sense of control for you in your current situation.

- **Aerobic Exercise:** Activities like running, cycling, and swimming increase heart rate and promote cardiovascular health, improving overall energy levels and resilience to stress.
- **Strength Training:** Building muscle through weight lifting or bodyweight exercises can improve physical health, supporting mental health by enhancing confidence and body image. This was true for me and in my experience, strength training exercises are those that have the greatest impact on your self image. You will feel stronger and you will be stronger.
- **Yoga and Mindfulness-Based Exercises:** These practices provide physical benefits and focus on breath control and meditation, helping to calm the mind and reduce anxiety.

Right now, when you focus on regular exercise and positive, healthy eating habits and become aware of how they assist your life, you can take this challenging time and reap the benefits in your physical and emotional well-being.

DEALING WITH EMOTIONAL EATING AND ALCOHOL

It would be easy for any man to begin unhealthy levels of drinking at the time of a marriage breakup, separation, or divorce. The same goes for unhealthy eating and living. I knew that immediately following my separation, I would be at risk of heading downhill extremely fast if I wasn't cautious about the food and drink I consumed. The separation resulted in the loss of my income and my home. I also had very little savings at the time. You have to agree that it was a pretty awful state to be in. I didn't want to take rock bottom and make it any lower!

You can stabilise your situation as I did and reduce the likelihood or impact of any negative behaviours in several ways.

Get some people on your team

Forget about handling it all yourself - no man is an island. Even Jesus had 12 disciples to help him! Right now, you just need some people close to you. Even two or three supportive friends or family will give you the encouragement and company you need to remain functional, maintain healthy habits and stay on track. If you can try to eat with others around a table, including your kids if you have them, it will help deter you from eating the wrong foods and drinking too much.

Create a whole new routine for a whole new you

My new daily routine was crucial to regaining my sense of normalcy, and a huge part of that was my exercise and meal planning. Creating a new routine that includes planning and preparing meals will help give you a sense of positive control and purpose. When you plan your food, you make healthier food choices. Learning to prepare simple, nutritious, tasty meals can also be therapeutic because, as I know, when you cook a great meal, especially for others, you will always get a fantastic sense of accomplishment.

Understand what's triggering you

Self-awareness is recognising the emotional triggers that lead to any of your bad habits. Once you identify them, you can seek healthier ways to cope with those emotions. My recommended recipe is a simple but powerful combination of routine cooking, exercise and healthy foods. Still, you can add anything, such as focusing on your interests or talking with a therapist.

Professionals are there for you, too

I didn't seek professional help from a counsellor or dietitian because I thought I was coping surprisingly well without those resources but mainly because I had no money to spare. However, your situation might be different. Mental and physical health professionals can be invaluable in helping you navigate the transition to healthier habits or keep you on track. Experts like NLP practitioners, psychologists and dieticians can offer personalised strategies and support for dealing with emotional eating, substance abuse and the challenges of adapting to a new lifestyle.

. . .

You get out what you put in

I'll keep making this point! Incorporating various nutrient-dense foods into your diet will improve your overall health and mood. Fruits, vegetables, whole grains, lean proteins and healthy fats provide the energy and nutrients necessary to handle stress more effectively. Additionally, consuming foods rich in omega-3 fatty acids, magnesium and B vitamins can support brain health and reduce symptoms of depression and anxiety. But it's more than food. Removing negative people and their negative inputs from your world is essential. Don't watch the news unless you want to feel depressed. Stay off socials. Don't put bad things in your brain. Stick to putting the good stuff in, and you'll keep the good results coming out.

Sweat more

I'll repeat this for everyone in the back row, too. Daily physical activity is a very effective way to reduce stress, improve your mood, maintain a healthy weight, or drop extra pounds. Exercise acts as a natural antidote to depression and anxiety (perhaps the best solution). It can also help reduce the temptation to overeat or abuse alcohol because it conflicts with your healthy identity.

Chill out and sleep more

Mindfulness practices, including mindful eating, can help us all become more attuned to our body's hunger and fullness signals, which is great because it reduces the likelihood of overeating and helps your enjoyment of eating. So sit there and enjoy the food you eat. Meditation can also alleviate stress and reduce the impulse to hit the bottle or eat more and you can find lots of free meditation apps on the app stores. While we're on the topic of chilling out, the other essential thing to remember is to get enough sleep. It's easy to get into a destructive sleep pattern immediately following a breakup. Sleeping can be tough when there is so much on your mind, or you might be reluctant to hit the hay because you are worried about the thoughts that might arise when you remove all other stimuli. I tackled this by being as disciplined as possible with a bedtime (10.30 pm) and by using a meditation app that would play sounds, including white noise (electric humming) or pink noise (environmental sounds like water, thunder and rain) or particular musical compositions at specific hertz levels that would slowly fill my brain and lull me into sleep. The most effective method I still use today is to play these types of sounds at a volume that barely registers in my ears but is still audible if I consciously listen. It quickly became a sound that was only registered unconsciously and I equate it to being like a slow, deep brain massage. This technique worked for me. I urge you to try it, too. It might take a few goes to find the sounds that work for you, but believe me, it's worth the effort.

Start learning new things

When you are no longer a married man, you suddenly have to build then adjust to, a new identity. I found it helpful to begin learning new things, as it helped me positively grow and fill a hole in my understanding of myself. I am naturally curious about many things, so rather than being on the negative treadmill of social media, I would use any time online to learn something. I had a wide variety of topics I began to study simply by watching YouTube videos. Some brilliant people are out there who are very open and generous with their knowledge. Because I wanted to improve myself and my communication skills, I learned about neurolinguistic programming (NLP) body language and Stoic principles. Because I was interested in political communications, I studied early to modern propaganda techniques. There was much more.

You could also learn anything new right now.

The entirety of the world's knowledge exists at your fingertips on the internet, much of it in video form. You also have AI to blow you away with instant answers to all your personal questions about any topic ever considered by anyone. It's truly an amazing time to learn, so take advantage of it. Think about your interests, and then make some time to watch your first learning video. Make this learning a habit, and soon, you will find you have new, positive dimensions to your identity, possibly even including new ways to improve your financial position.

The recipe for renewed strength

Taking the chance to adopt healthier habits in the wake of your divorce or separation, as I did, is not just about your physical health. It's about rebuilding and renewing yourself from the inside out. By focusing on nourishment, looking after yourself, and developing positive coping mechanisms, I promise you can emerge from this difficult period in your life as a stronger, healthier and more resilient person.

I know that at this time in your life, it is very easy to get depleted and depressed and to stop looking after yourself.

You are not going to let that happen to you.

You owe it to yourself, at the very least, and anyone else you care about to look after yourself. You now have the opportunity to be different and to be even better. Don't be defined by the past or the ideas of others. You can start the process of developing the new you now.

You have the guide right here to follow to ensure your mind and body remain fully operational and regain strength. The good news is that you will notice that it's basic and easy and when you follow the guide, you will see the results like I did. You feel better about yourself, and you keep going. You improve, and so you keep going. This becomes a positive feedback loop and adds to your motivation and determination.

Can you imagine how great you can look and feel in just a few weeks?

I've always been into nutrition. Before I became a Chef, I completed a one-year pre-apprenticeship course (Chef School) and part of my study was Food Science. I loved the subject and became the equal top of the class for the year. That was some handy knowledge, and so immediately following my separation, I worked out what basic foods I needed to survive and operate and build myself up to be better than ever. I then had a guide for my shopping.

The following is that guide, my cheat sheet of basic ingredients and a range of foods that you will need that are healthy and flexible in the ways you can use and cook with them.

The lists here are what I followed in my kitchen operation planning, and in each case, you don't need to run out and get everything I've listed. I know that sometimes, for whatever reason, this will not be possible for you because the same applied to me. So that's ok. Don't stress. Just get what you can or what you are comfortable with at the time. The main thing is that overall, you are looking after your health and well-being in an informed way with a great diet that is tasty, diverse and nutritious.

CHAPTER 9
THE FOOD BASICS YOU NEED

"THE DOCTOR OF THE FUTURE WILL NO LONGER TREAT THE HUMAN FRAME WITH DRUGS, BUT RATHER WILL CURE AND PREVENT DISEASE WITH NUTRITION."

THOMAS EDISON

In this section of the book, I outline the basic ingredients you will need in the kitchen and why they are good for you. We will look at fresh foods, herbs and spices, canned foods and dry goods, their uses in cooking and nutritional value for you.

We'll start in the freezer and take it from there.

Fresh is best but frozen can be pretty bloody good too.

Of course I'm a huge advocate for fresh food, but sometimes it's impossible to get certain items; other times, having some prepared frozen foods in the freezer is a lifesaver.

Image: This is how AI decides to show a whole range of frozen vegetables, when you ask it. Bit weird. At least it tried.

The following list highlights nutritionally valuable foods and excellent healthy choices for you and anyone else you might need to feed or look after when fresh produce isn't an option. Ideally, you will have this mix of fruit and veggies each week, as the different colours provide different levels of vitamins and minerals, but just grab what you can. I understand that cost and time are issues for all of us.

Broccoli: You'll probably love it or hate it. But it's damn good for you. It's high in vitamins C and K and a good source of fibre and antioxidants. (We discuss fresh broccoli later).

Spinach: Why was Popeye so strong? (This is an old reference - please search it up if you don't know what the hell I'm on about). Anyway, it's packed with iron, calcium, and vitamins A, C, and K and cooks super fast. This is another one we will discuss later.

Peas: Despite how cruel it sounds, I prefer baby peas, but really, any peas are great. They're rich in vitamins A, C, K, and B vitamins, as well as protein and fibre.

Green Beans: I have to admit I don't like these, but you can hide them in dishes and you never have to taste them. They are a good source of fibre, Vitamin C and folate.

Brussels Sprouts: These are better fresh, as freezing them adds a bit too much liquid for the way I like to cook them, but like the green beans, we can hide the frozen Brussel Sprouts in certain dishes and get their benefits that way. They are high in vitamins C and K, fibre and contain antioxidants.

Cauliflower: There's a lot you can do with cauliflower, and like some other vegetables in this list, it can be successfully hidden in a recipe so its flavour is not so apparent or is masked if you're not that into it. Getting this into you will give you the benefit of vitamins C and K and fibre.

Corn: Is there anyone who doesn't love corn? This is a great one if you have kids or just in general! Corn is a good source of fibre and B vitamins and has the benefit of being filling too.

Soy Beans (Edamame): With soybeans, we have got ourselves an excellent and tasty source of plant-based protein, fibre and various vitamins and minerals.

Mango: As I always say, *man goes* to the freezer when seeking a delicious snack. Actually, I've never said that; it's ridiculous. In any case, mangoes are delicious, rich in vitamins A and C, and perfect for smoothies, salsas and any tropical-themed desserts you might want to make.

Mixed berries: Berry good for you! (Sorry.)

A typical frozen berry mix you can find at the supermarket includes blueberries, strawberries, raspberries and blackberries. This combination is fantastic - it's a total powerhouse of vitamins and minerals, making it an incredibly nutritious addition to your diet. I'm giving the berries a lot of time here as they are the only frozen fruit on my list and will be very valuable for you. You can turn them into all kinds of different healthy foods and snacks.

Just check out all the vitamins and minerals in this mix of berries and why they are so good for you:

- *Vitamin C*: Particularly high in strawberries, it's an essential vitamin, important for immune function, skin health and iron absorption.

- *Vitamin K*: Found in all these berries, especially in blackberries, Vitamin K is crucial for blood clotting and bone health.
- *Vitamin A*: All these berries, but particularly blackberries and blueberries, contain Vitamin A, which is vital for eye health, immune function and skin health.
- *Folate (Vitamin B9)*: Essential for DNA synthesis and repair, cell division and growth. Berries, especially strawberries, are a good source of folate.
- *Manganese*: Particularly high in raspberries and blackberries, manganese is essential for bone development and nutrient metabolism.
- *Fibre*: All these berries are high in dietary fibre, which is beneficial for digestive health and can help manage blood sugar levels.
- *Antioxidants*: Berries are famous for their high antioxidant content, including flavonoids, anthocyanins, and ellagic acid which can help fight inflammation and oxidative stress. Studies have shown that these guys can help assist against Cancer.
- *Potassium*: Important for heart and muscle function and found in moderate amounts in these berries.
- *Magnesium*: Essential for muscle and nerve function, magnesium is present in these fruits, with blackberries being an excellent source.
- *Calcium*: While not in high amounts, berries contribute some calcium important for strong and healthy bones.

How good are mixed berries, right?

NOW CHECK YOUR OIL

Next on our list of basic foods and ingredients you need to ensure you're healthy and which help build your strength are oils. As I said before, you don't need to run out and get all these, but if you have them around, they will give you more flavour and meal options.

Image: When you ask AI to show you different bottles and types of oil in a kitchen, it develops a hipster multi-oil brand with an organic vibe and unusual mis-spellings.

Extra Virgin Olive Oil

Get this one, if nothing else. It's my number one. I use litres of this stuff in my cooking for all kinds of reasons. It's delicious, adaptable and most importantly, extra virgin olive oil has amazing health benefits. It's been shown to be effective against strokes, heart disease and cancer, among its other superpowers.

Canola Oil

Canola Oil is not a show pony oil. It's basic, neutral flavoured oil and not particularly tasty. However, it is good for various cooking needs, including sautéing (if you don't have olive oil) and shallow frying, as it has a high smoke point (this just means you can heat it up a lot before you see smoke from the pan). If you can't get Canola oil, try Sunflower oil, which is similar. Note: some research says Seed Oils are bad. You might want to check on that.

Coconut Oil

It's not a thing I use all the time, but when I do, I love cooking with coconut oil. It's highly versatile due to its stability at high temperatures (that high smoke point again), making it suitable for frying, sautéing, and baking. It's often also used in vegan cooking as a substitute for butter since it is rich and tends to solidify easily.

You need to remember that it does taste like coconut (surprise, surprise!) so when you use it, you will get that distinct flavour. This means you may not want to use it for everything, but you can add a tropical twist to your dishes when appropriate.

Avocado Oil

This one is a pretty good substitute for Olive Oil if you want a change. It has many similar health benefits and you can use it in several ways too, including high-heat cooking methods like frying and grilling. Its taste is slightly nutty, so it can add flavour without overpowering your other ingredients. If you can't get this one, try Grape-seed oil.

Sesame Oil

Sesame oil is a common Asian ingredient that usually comes in a small bottle as the flavour is quite strong and concentrated. Normally, you will only use a few drops in a dish to get the flavour benefits of this oil. There are two types you might find - light and dark. While they both have a distinct flavour, the dark version has a stronger taste.

HERBS AND SPICES

People often get confused with herbs and spices and it's easy to see why. They think you need to add these things to your dishes to give them 'flavour'. That's not entirely true. The thing that adds the most flavour to your meals will very often be *the cooking method itself*. Using herbs and spices correctly gives a great extra dimension to your food without overwhelming the flavour. The trick is knowing which ones to use and in what quantities.

Basic herbs to have around

The world is full of all sorts of amazing delicious herbs we can use in our cooking. For now, and for your purposes, I'm keeping this list short and basic, just like the recipes in this book. You don't need a full array of herbs, just the ones that will be most adaptable and useful for your needs.

Please remember to WASH ALL YOUR HERBS (and fruit and veggies, for that matter) as they will often have small but highly unsatisfying amounts of dirt in amongst their herby goodness and a meal that includes dirt is not the way to delight your taste buds or make friends.

Basil

I worked with a French chef who called Basil "The King of Herbs", and I could see why. Basil is adaptable across many dishes and cuisines, including Italian and Southeast Asian. It has a great sweet, slightly peppery flavour. When it's fresh, you can use it to add a burst of flavour to all kinds of dishes like pastas and salads, and turn it into 'pesto.' Its aromatic qualities also make it a popular garnish, elevating the sensory appeal of dishes. If you can't get it fresh, dried basil can be used for convenience and shelf life in many dishes, particularly slow-cooked meals. If that is not enough for you, Basil also has health benefits, including anti-inflammatory and antibacterial properties.

Image: This AI image of basil and coriander in a market is actually pretty good.

Coriander (Cilantro)

When I was an apprentice chef and I first came across Coriander, I hated it. The smell reminded me of squashed garden beetles and actually made me want to vomit.

Ok, I'll start again. I got over that initial disgust somehow, mainly through exposure I think, and started to love its clean freshness and distinct flavour. Now I use the fresh leaves, stems, and dried seeds in my cooking all the time, particularly across Mexican, Middle Eastern and Asian-inspired dishes. Fresh coriander is an integral ingredient in salads, salsas and curries. The seeds have this warm, slightly citrusy and earthy taste and are either ground into a spice or used whole in pickling, baking or seasoning in meat and vegetable dishes. Its bonus health benefits include aiding digestion and its antioxidant properties. Please note that you should wash your Coriander before you use it as it often has small amounts of gritty soil and dirt on the leaves and stems and if ANY of that gets in your food, it will spoil the whole meal.

Parsley

Like Basil, Parsley is a great all-rounder, very adaptable in cooking and used across many dishes. It has a fresh, slightly bitter taste. There are two types you normally buy fresh: flat leaf and curly. The flat version is the milder version, with the curly type having a stronger bitterness. The flavour profiles might be different in different parts of the world so just test it yourself. Parsley is a staple in Mediterranean cuisine and can be found in traditional salads, soups and dishes like tabbouleh and chimichurri. It's also used in a lot of European cooking, in meals including pasta, roasts, and stews. Dried parsley can be used as a fresh substitute for some meals if none is available. As a bonus, Parsley is also packed with vitamins and antioxidants that help fight cancer and free radicals, so it's good for you too!

Rosemary

Rosemary is one of the stronger herbs, so you need to be careful how much of it you use in your cooking. It has a powerful aroma and flavour, almost pine-like. It's used often in Mediterranean cuisine, slow-cooked meals, traditional roasted vegetables, and meats like lamb, pork and chicken. There are also lots of examples of its use in soups, breads and doughs such as pizza bases. When it is fresh, you cut it up finely with a large sharp knife, and I suggest that once it is chopped up, you add small amounts and test the flavour when including it in meals. It is slightly stronger when dried and can be added to meals in any form. Like many of the other herbs listed here, Rosemary has great potential health benefits, helping ward off nasty colds and reducing inflammation in the body.

Image: I think this AI image of oregano, sage and rosemary is quite a good effort too.

Thyme

Thyme is a great, adaptable herb I use quite often, and it works well with a range of others. It has a pleasant aroma and a slightly minty, earthy flavour that matches nicely with numerous other flavours and dishes, including soups, stews, roasts, marinades and sauces. You prepare Thyme by stripping the small leaves from their woody stems and chopping them up finely, and you will see it used in lots of European cuisine, particularly Mediterranean, Italian, and French cooking. Both fresh and dried thyme is used in cooking, with fresh thyme having a less concentrated flavour. A variation on Thyme is Lemon Thyme which as the name suggests, has the addition of a lemony flavour, which is excellent in poultry dishes along with Sage. Thyme is commonly added early in the cooking process, allowing its oils and aroma to permeate the dish. Once again, Thyme is another herb with medicinal properties (even as an antimicrobial) and high antioxidant content.

Mint

Mint, as I'm sure you know, is a refreshing, aromatic herb, with a cool, sweet and sometimes peppery flavour, widely used in both food and drink preparations, especially prominent in Middle Eastern and Mediterranean dishes. There is a range of types, including peppermint, apple mint and spearmint. Mint's versatility allows for its use in a variety of ways: as a fresh garnish for desserts and drinks, infused in teas and cocktails and as a key ingredient in salads, sauces like mint chutney and dishes such as tabbouleh. Its bright crisp flavour pairs well with fruits, lamb, poultry and peas. Beyond all that, mint is great for digestion and soothing an anxious or nauseous stomach, and it's often used for these purposes and as a natural breath freshener. It is more for the medicinal purpose of mint that I have included it in this list for you. Mint tea will assist your mental and physical well-being when you're seeking to feel more calm and settled. Fresh mint is much better in my opinion, as you get the full benefit of the flavour and aroma but dried mint can also be used in limited cases and recipes.

Image: AI nailed this close-up image of early morning mint at the fruit and vegetable market.

THE SPICE OF LIFE

Add just enough spice to your new life with this list. I've chosen these spices for their versatility, easy accessibility (ie. I'm not listing super bloody rare Wild Tibetan Mountain Peppers that only occur under six feet of snow above 26,000 feet for three days of the year) and their health benefits.

Salt

Ok! I know Salt is a *mineral, not a spice*, but I'm adding it anyway, as it sits naturally with a list of spices and gets along very well with everyone else around here. There are a range of different types including rock salt, Himalayan Pink Salt (not super rare), table salt and others. They all do the same thing: enhance the flavour of whatever they're added to. For simplicity I suggest purchasing Iodised Sea Salt, but any of them will do. The addition of iodine in your diet is essential to health, explaining why it's added to something used every day like salt. Iodine helps assist metabolism, growth, and development in the human body for all of us - from unborn babies to adults.

Black Pepper

Along with salt, Black Pepper is probably the most common seasoning you'll find in kitchens across the world. Made from the dried berries of the Piper nigrum plant, black pepper appears in several forms: whole, cracked, kibbled and ground. Like salt, you can pretty much add it to anything you like, according to your tastes.

Cumin

Cumin is a warm, earthy spice with a unique savoury flavour profile and a slightly bitter undertone. You'll find it used extensively in curries, soups, stews and chilli recipes from Middle Eastern, Indian, Latin American and North African regions. Derived from the dried seeds of the Cuminum cyminum plant, it's a key ingredient in many spice blends such as curry powder and garam masala. Often I will use cumin alongside its close friends; fresh or ground coriander and chilli. In addition to its culinary uses, cumin is also known for its digestive properties (good for the stomach parts!). As such, it is used in traditional medicines for those essential gut health benefits.

Image: This is my mind's eye idea of a Middle Eastern spice shop and it's AI's as well. Glad we agree on this.

Paprika

I love using different types of Paprika, including sweet, hot and smoked versions. A rich red powder that adds appealing colour and flavour to dishes, Paprika is vibrant, flavourful, and made from ground sweet and hot dried red bell peppers (also called 'capsicums' in some regions). It originates from the Capsicum annuum plant species and is a staple in Hungarian, Spanish, and Moroccan cooking, used in stews (like the classic Hungarian dish Goulash, which is fantastic and delicious) and soups and rubs for meats. In Spanish cooking, paprika is used to make two other things I love: Chorizo (sausages) and Paella.

Turmeric

This is another one that makes the list because it is not only commonly used in many dishes and combined with other spices, but it also has fantastic health benefits for you in all its different forms. Turmeric is a beautiful bright yellow with a warm, bitter taste and earthy aroma. In cooking, it's typically used as a powder and key ingredient in curry mixes, but you can also use fresh turmeric root when you can find it. Its distinct colour gives a rich golden hue to dishes, making it a favourite in rice dishes, soups and sauces but you will need to be careful about how much you use when working with it - you do not want to add too much and destroy your creation. Like ginger, Turmeric is well known for its fantastic anti-inflammatory and antioxidant properties and is used in lots of traditional medicines with great effect.

Cinnamon

Since I was a little kid, Cinnamon has been my favourite spice. I love the spicy aroma and the woody sweetness and flavour. I was fascinated that it was made from bark - the inner bark of the Cinnamomum genus tree to be precise. It is available as little 'sticks' or ground finely to be used in food and drinks for both its flavour and health properties. There are thousands of sweet dishes and foods that use Cinnamon as a key ingredient, including pastries, desserts, and hot beverages like Egg Nog where it adds a warm, comforting flavour. It also has plenty of uses in savoury cooking, particularly in Middle Eastern and Indian cuisines, where it adds depth and warmth to curries, stews and rice dishes.

Garlic Powder

I use garlic in almost everything, and not just to ward off the Vampires at the door. It's a great flavour addition and it has significant health benefits. Garlic powder is the dry variation made from dehydrated ground garlic. It's good to have in the cupboard because it's convenient and provides the versatility and flavour of garlic in a concentrated form. You can just throw it into a wide range of dishes from all four corners of the world without the work required to peel and chop fresh garlic. I use it in many ways, including seasoning blends, marinades, rubs and sauces. It's sweeter than fresh garlic so it gives a more subtle garlic flavour. Because it is very fine, garlic powder blends well in spice mixes and is excellent in dry rubs for meats.

Image: AI decided it wanted Rembrandt lighting and a Renaissance Master's still life twist for this image of garlic, ginger and turmeric root. Good job.

Ginger Powder

Ginger can divide people, but I love it in all foods. Ginger powder is more subtle than fresh ginger, and has a warm, spicy, and slightly sweet flavour with a similar fine texture to garlic powder and will often be used alongside it in spice mixes, curry powders and masalas. It's a common ingredient in a variety of cuisines, especially in Asian, Indian and Middle Eastern dishes. Of course, it is also a key ingredient in gingerbread and other sweet cookies, spice cakes and desserts where fresh ginger would be too overpowering. Ginger powder also has many well-known medicinal properties both as a preventative and a component of treatments, especially for colds and cases of flu, so make sure you get some into your body regularly.

Chilli Powder

Bring some Tex-Mex heat to your cooking! You might recall I was a fan of Hot Tabasco Sauce before I finished primary school, so I am naturally including Chilli in the list here. Plus, it adds a great dimension to your meals, assuming you can handle it! The intensity and flavour of chilli powder can vary greatly depending on the types of chillies used, ranging from mild to extremely hot. So just make sure you know which one you are getting. A Chilli powder blend can add heat and depth to classic dishes such as Chilli Con Carne, but also stews, sauces, marinades and rubs.

Chilli powder can also boost metabolism and even help in pain relief due to its capsaicin content.

Image: Another great spice market image and some serious food styling by AI.

Nutmeg

Nutmeg is like the almost twin brother of Cinnamon because they share many characteristics. For example it also has a warm, sweet, spicy flavour with a similar woodiness that comes from the fact that Nutmeg is also a tree product - the brown seed of the Myristica fragrans tree. It's used across myriad cuisines including Indian, Middle Eastern and European, particularly in Italian and Dutch cooking. Like Cinnamon, nutmeg adds depth and warmth in sweet recipes such as pastries, puddings and spice cakes. It's also added to drinks like eggnog and mulled wine. In savoury dishes, nutmeg enhances the flavour of sauces like the French béchamel (cheese) sauce. Available both ground and as a whole seed, nutmeg is often grated fresh to preserve its aromatic oils. Like many other spices and foods I have listed here, it also has beneficial anti-inflammatory and digestive properties.

Curry Powder

As the name suggests, Curry Powder is the basis of (surprise, surprise) - curries. It can be made from a diverse variety of spices depending on the type of curry dish you are making, but as a general rule a standard curry powder will include fenugreek, coriander powder, cumin, mustard powder, onion powder, salt, chilli powder, turmeric, garlic powder, black or white pepper and ginger powder. The versatility of curry powder means it has uses beyond traditional curries, adding an exotic or spicy twist to everyday home cooking. (Remember curried egg sandwiches?) Curry powder is a great way to quickly add a complex array of flavours and aromas to your dish - just watch out how much you add! The best approach is a little at a time until you reach a flavour you're happy with.

WHAT'S IN THE PANTRY?

So now we have our basic seasonings, herbs and frozen foods sorted, let's get to the most nutritious and tasty dried foods and pantry staples you need to give you the range of ingredients required to make awesome foods quickly and easily without having to be a five-star chef or spending hours in the kitchen.

Quinoa

I used to think that when rice goes to the gym to get shredded, that's Quinoa. You'd also be forgiven for not really knowing what this ingredient is because it has only recently become "a thing" in kitchens worldwide. Now I know that Quinoa is a highly nutritious grain-like seed with a nutty flavour and a slightly crunchy texture. It has exploded in popularity as a superfood because of its high protein content and rich supply of essential amino acids, fibre, vitamins and minerals. It is indigenous to the Andean region of South America and is used as a healthier substitute for rice and other grains. It's hugely versatile and can be served as a side dish, added to salads for extra texture, used in soups and stews and incorporated into baking for a nutritional boost. Additionally, it's gluten-free, making it an excellent option for those with gluten sensitivities. Easy to prepare and adaptable to many flavours, quinoa has become a go-to ingredient for health-conscious cooks and those looking to diversify their dietary choices. Because of all these factors, everyone, including vegetarians and vegans, loves it.

Brown Rice

While it has a great nutty flavour, one of the things I love most about Brown Rice is its chewy texture. It's just so satisfying to eat! It's a whole grain rice which means it retains its bran and germ layers so it's more nutritious than white rice and a rich source of dietary fibre, vitamins and minerals like magnesium and selenium. It has the position of a well-earned staple in health-conscious diets (which is why it's here!) and has the adaptability to be the basis of a whole meal like a soup, casserole or stir fry, or a wholesome side dish or base in salads and pilaffs. Brown rice takes longer to cook than white rice, but so what - put it on a little earlier! You'll thank me, and so will your body.

Hemp Powder

Hemp powder is another superfood made from ground hemp seeds. I like its nutty taste and add it to breakfasts like porridge and smoothies because of its fantastic nutritional profile. It's a complete protein which means it contains all nine essential amino acids. These are great for overall strength and health and for energy and muscle repair when exercising. The powder is rich in omega-3 and omega-6 fatty acids and supports heart health by improving cholesterol levels and reducing inflammation. Because it has a high fibre content, it's excellent for digestive health and weight management because you will feel full for longer. Vegans and vegetarians are big fans because of all these qualities and of course, the fact that it is plant-based too.

Chia

For ages, I had no idea about Chia seeds. I only really knew them from their appearances in fancy breakfast bowls at cafes. But when I decided to stop drinking coffee, I researched how to gain quick energy in the morning and Chia (along with hemp powder and a few other things) came up as a recommendation and a great addition to my diet. And immediately, I became a convert. Chia seeds are a tiny but mighty powerhouse of nutritional goodness! Native to Central America, they are full of omega-3 fatty acids, so they're excellent for heart health because they lower your blood pressure and reduce bad cholesterol. They are also a fantastic source of fibre and are full of protein, calcium, magnesium and phosphorus, all of which help your energy levels and body repair functions. Throw a handful of these nutty-flavoured seeds into pretty much anything you like, including smoothies, yoghurt, porridge or baked goods. When they are immersed in a liquid over time (for example, overnight), they expand and become large, semi-transparent balls with (in my opinion) a very pleasing gel-like texture.

Lentils

Lentils are a type of legume that are amazingly good for you and can be bought canned or dry in most supermarkets. They have a reputation for being the basis of a hippie, vegetarian diet as they are commonly cheap to buy, easy to cook, and highly nutritious. As a food for the classic university student persona - they are perfect. Well, the same goes for the rest of us. Lentils are a great source of protein, fibre and essential nutrients like iron and folate, making them a staple in vegetarian and vegan diets for all people. They come in various colours, including brown, green, red, and black, each with its own texture and cooking time. You can use lentils in lots of meal types, from hearty soups and stews to salads and side dishes. In Indian cooking, lentils are a key ingredient in dal's and curries, seasoned with aromatic spices. In the Middle East, they form the basis of dishes like Mujaddara. Canned lentils have a short cooking time (10 to 15 minutes approximately) and don't need to be pre-cooked (like other legumes), making them extra convenient when you're busy and time-poor. Dried ones require 30 to 40 minutes or a bit less if you soak them overnight. Whether they are the dried or canned variety, the earthy flavour of lentils absorbs seasonings well, allowing them to blend harmoniously with various other ingredients, making them a versatile, tasty and healthy choice in your kitchen.

Canned Tomatoes

I'm almost certain that everyone's mum has used these and has a couple of cans handy and ready to go right now. There are excellent reasons for this. Canned tomatoes are a staple in kitchens worldwide because they are so convenient and versatile and last forever in the cupboard. They come in various forms, including whole, diced, crushed, tomato paste, or a smooth sauce called Passata. Canned tomatoes are essential in dishes where fresh tomatoes are hard to come by or when a deeper, more concentrated tomato flavour is desired. They have many uses across sauces, soups, stews, pasta meals and casseroles. Italian dishes, including pizzas and lasagnas, often rely on canned tomatoes to add a rich and robust flavour to the base since the canning process actually enhances the natural sweetness and taste appeal of tomatoes. Canned tomatoes are also a key ingredient in Mexican salsas, Indian curries and classic American chilli. And if that's not enough, mums can throw them at people when they totally lose it.

Tinned Tuna

Tinned tuna is a brilliant addition tc the pantry for many reasons. I prefer the tinned tuna in olive oil just because it combines the health benefits and flavours of tuna with olive oil in a single package and it's a better choice than tuna in water if you want to cook it as little as the oil helps it fry in the pan. Tuna is packed with goodness, including high-quality protein, essential omega-3 fatty acids, vitamins D and B12, and minerals like selenium and iodine. It helps your heart, your muscle development, your brain and your immune system all at once! The olive oil also brings its benefits to the party too. You can use tinned tuna in plenty of dishes such as salads, sandwiches, pasta bakes and more. It's hugely convenient when you're busy but want a quick, inexpensive, nutritious and tasty meal. Gotta love that!

Almonds

Almonds are easy to love, too. There are plenty of ways to use them, they're nutritious and they're added to all kinds of recipes across the world in including desserts, for their delicate, slightly sweet flavour and crunchy texture. They are rich in healthy fats, protein, fibre and vitamin E. They can be pummelled into almond flour for gluten-free baking, ground up for marzipan, macarons and other desserts or slivered, adding crunch to salads, rice dishes and stir-fries. You've probably seen, heard of or consumed almond milk too, which has gained huge popularity as a dairy-free alternative to cow's milk. If that's not enough, there's even almond butter, a nut-spread alternative to the usual peanut butter. Their ability to enhance many dishes' flavour and nutritional profile makes almonds a top ingredient choice for me.

Oats

When we think of oats, it's probably as a breakfast food like porridge, oatmeal and granola. But oats are also used in recipes for cookies, muffins and bread and as a useful way to thicken soups and stews. They have an almost sweet, nutty flavour and come in forms (with varying textures), including whole oat groats, steel-cut oats, rolled oats and quick oats, each varying in texture and cooking time. Oats are high in fibre, great for digestion and heart health. They also contribute to lower cholesterol levels and provide sustained energy, making them a staple ingredient in diets focused on health and wellness - hence why they're here on our list.

Honey

What an amazing product the bees produce! It's easy to forget how incredible honey is since it's such a common food item, and ever since I was a kid, I have been fascinated with its flavours, colours, texture, and uses. There is a massive variety of honey since its flavour is related to the type of bee, regional and climatic variations such as the flowers and pollen and the season it is produced in. Whatever the type, it is renowned for its rich, sweet taste and health benefits. In cooking, honey is used across almost anything you might eat, adding a level of sweetness and moisture to dishes, ranging from baked goods and sauces to dressings and marinades and drinks such as tea. Its health benefits are extraordinary, too. Honey has been used in traditional medicine for centuries, especially as a natural remedy for coughs and as a component in skincare treatments. It has antioxidant properties, potential anti-inflammatory effects, and ability to soothe sore throats. Specific honey types such as Manuka Honey are said to have even stronger positive impacts on health and well-being. A big thank you to the bees!

Balsamic Vinegar

I love this stuff. How much? Well, this is the kind of vinegar I chugged from the bottle when I was a kid, hiding in the pantry with the door closed. Balsamic Vinegar is a distinctive, dark vinegar that has a reputation for being a gourmet product, and that reputation is well deserved. Originating from Italy, it is a richly flavoured vinegar made from aged and fermented grape must. It has a complex, sweet and tangy flavour which makes it great for adding depth and distinct taste to various dishes. As a vinegar, it has its standard use in salad dressings, but there are plenty of other uses. For example, it is also great for marinades and glazes to enhance the flavours of all kinds of meats, vegetables and fruits. You can throw it on top of some hot grilled vegetables, add it to a Napoli sauce, and even use it in desserts. Balsamic vinegar is valued not only for all its uses in the kitchen but also for its potential health benefits for your blood circulation, as an antioxidant and digestive aid. And I was secretly drinking it by the bottle by the time I was five!

Dried Beans

Dried beans is not a term that relates to one particular type of bean; it can relate to different varieties of beans, such as kidney beans, black beans, cannellini beans, pinto beans and chickpeas. All these beans have their unique tastes and textures, suitable for many cooking applications. Whatever dried beans we might use, they are an excellent source of protein, fibre, vitamins and minerals. They also help maintain healthy blood sugar levels, improve heart health, and support digestive health. You can see why they are a popular choice in both health-conscious diets and vegetarian and vegan diets (as a meat alternative). For these reasons, cultures worldwide use dried beans in cooking a wide array of dishes, including soups, stews, salads, dips and casseroles. For preparation, they must first be soaked and then cooked, which enhances their digestibility and flavour. Along with all these great benefits, dried beans are affordable, have an extremely long shelf life, and are easy to store and discover in supermarkets everywhere. What's not to love!?

Whole Wheat Pasta

Just like you have white bread and the healthier versions of wholemeal or wholegrain bread, or white rice or brown rice, you can also get a healthier version of the standard pasta you might use. This is whole wheat pasta and it's made from the whole wheat grain, including the outer husk or shell, not just the carbohydrate-rich centre. Because of this, it stands out for its higher fibre, protein, vitamins and minerals, hence its place in a balanced and health-conscious diet. I will often use any form of whole wheat pasta to replace any regular pasta in a recipe from spaghetti and meatballs to lasagne or a light pasta salad. The whole grain gives it an appealing nutty flavour and firm texture (similar to brown rice) that adds a distinctive twist to your dishes. For health benefits, the increased fibre content helps your digestion and makes you feel full and satisfied. If that's not enough, it helps you maintain stable blood sugar levels, so it's an excellent choice if you have diabetes or want to maintain a healthy weight.

A FEW OTHER FRESH INGREDIENTS

Before we move on, I just want to add a couple of other fresh food items here that are awesome to have around for various reasons and that you should strongly consider adding to your new diet.

Natural Greek Yoghurt

Natural Greek Yoghurt is a food that contains millions and millions of live bacteria that your body loves. I found out this when I was a kid and I thought it was super cool that when I ate yoghurt millions of these little guys entered my stomach and digestive system to take care of business and keep me healthy. It was slightly bizarre to think all these things were inside me running around doing a job like that, but I appreciated the effort. I also loved the tangy flavour and the creamy texture. But there is more to love. Apart from the probiotics (the guys in my stomach), natural Greek yogurt is nutrient-rich in other ways and is an excellent source of protein for muscle building and calcium for bone strength. You can eat it with fruit or use it across all types of dishes, including breakfast bowls, smoothies, dips and as a substitute for sour cream or mayonnaise in some recipes. This type of yoghurt also contains less lactose than traditional yoghurt, so it's easier to digest if you are lactose intolerant.

Firm Tofu

There are different types of tofu but the one that I'd suggest you buy and keep in the fridge is Firm Tofu. You will normally find it in the supermarket in the open fridge area near the cheese and fresh pasta. Note that it's usually not called 'firm tofu' on the packet; it's just tofu. When you pick it up you will notice its weight and firm texture. Tofu is made from soybeans and water and a coagulant that keeps the whole thing together. It's excellent for both nutrition and versatility in the kitchen.

Soybeans contain high-quality plant-based protein, which is why you hear vegetarians and vegans going on about Tofu all the time as a great meat substitute. It's also low on calories and rich in essential amino acids, iron, calcium and other minerals that keep you healthy in many ways, from how your blood works to your bone health and overall wellbeing. Because of its fairly neutral flavour and sponginess, Tofu can absorb all kinds of flavours particularly well so it tends to be put into marinades before cooking. And to top it off, it's incredibly adaptable - great for stir-fries, grilling and baking, vegetarian tacos, burgers and soups.

Beetroot

I bet that Beetroot is not a vegetable that is top of mind when you go shopping. But you should keep it in mind. It's extremely good for you, tastes great and you can use it in multiple ways. Fresh beetroot is a vibrant, deep, red root vegetable with what I consider to be a sweet earthy flavour. Like all the deep red and purple fruits and vegetables, it's packed with vitamin C and antioxidants, so it has that powerful anti-cancer and immune-boosting property. It's also full of vitamin B9 (folate) and fibre and includes essential minerals like potassium and manganese. It helps you maintain healthy blood pressure, is great for your digestion, and is packed with nitrates, which enhance blood flow and help improve your athletic performance. How good is that? Beetroot really does assist your body all over the place. For these reasons, plus the taste, I regularly add beetroot to my diet in various forms such as pickled or raw (usually grated) in salads, as a drink, and slowly roasted (which draws out even more sweetness).

Kiwifruit

I had to squeeze this guy in. I mean, how can you not respect a fruit that can grow its own hair? Kiwifruit are a delicious self-contained snack with a thin, fuzzy skin covering flesh that's either green or golden filled with tiny black seeds. The flavour of ripe Kiwifruit is both tangy and sweet and packs a mighty health punch with some unusual properties to boot. For example, you will be surprised to know that Kiwi's have even more vitamin C than oranges, so immediately they are fantastic for your immune system. But that's just the start. They are a low-calorie snack that enhances skin health through collagen production and they contain a unique enzyme called actinidin that can help break down proteins. This means that not only is it a nutritious addition to smoothies and fruit salads, Kiwifruit is also an excellent tenderiser for meat as well! Who would have thought? Want more? You got it! Kiwifruit has high potassium content, which helps manage your blood pressure levels and its antioxidants protect you from free radicals, which are nasty elements that cause cancer. All that goodness in this quirky little hairy, dark green thing. Go get some now. I prefer the Gold Kiwifruit myself but the green variety are great too.

Lemon

When you go on a boat trip for a few months at sea, remember to take these. We all know that lemons are basically Vitamin C in a thick yellow skin, and way back in the day, Sailors knew that too. They ate lemons while on long voyages to prevent a disease called Scurvy (a particularly old-fashioned name for a disease, don't you think?). The reason it's old-fashioned is because it's a vintage ailment and none of us get Scurvy anymore because we eat things high in Vitamin C, like lemons. Genius! But there are lots more reasons to keep lemons around. The flavour of lemon is almost universally loved, and lemons are used across all types of cuisine. We can sweeten it and make a drink like lemonade or a dessert, and we can add it to savoury dishes to provide a satisfying tang. You can combine it with honey, team and ginger to assist with your cold and flu management and it can work as a tasty tenderiser in marinades to break down proteins in meats and seafood.

Kale / Spinach / Broccoli

The dense green and leafy things. We already have some of these in the freezer but you do need the fresh stuff too.

Kale, Spinach and Broccoli are the three green vegetables that arguably share the title for healthiest green vegetables. Identifying the single green vegetable with the most health benefits is challenging because each offers their own unique nutrient profile and health advantages. It's a pretty close call so I've included them all. You only have to pick one!

Ex-President of the USA, George HW Bush, once famously said he hated broccoli and he would not eat it even if it "was served on a silver platter", and all the broccoli farmers went crazy about it. I know why they went crazy because getting the kids to eat their broccoli is hard enough, let alone when the President says it's totally cool not to! I think Bush should have stuck with it a bit more. Broccoli is a powerful vegetable.

Broccoli stands out in the vegetable world because it is packed with goodness of all kinds. It's rich in vitamins C and K, folate, fibre and minerals like potassium and manganese. It's also loaded with bioactive compounds and antioxidants, such as sulforaphane, which research has indicated have genuine potential to reduce the risk of lots of awful things like heart disease, certain cancers and inflammatory conditions. The high fibre content in broccoli is also great for your gut health and digestion processes. It's a very adaptable vegetable in cooking and it can have a particularly satisfying crunch. But hey, if you don't like it, you have two other choices, just like the Ex-President does.

Kale and spinach.

Like broccoli, these two green vegetables are great in many foods, are incredibly nutrient-dense and each has its own health benefits. But between these two it's quite hard to declare one as definitively "stronger" than the other regarding those health benefits.

Let's put them head to head.

In the green corner, we have the self-consciously trendy powerhouse, Kale:

- Kale is high in vitamins A, C, and K and it has more of these vitamins per serving than spinach. That's a good start.
- It contains more fibre too, which is beneficial for digestive health.
- Kale also has higher levels of antioxidants such as quercetin and kaempferol, which have anti-inflammatory and anti-viral properties.
- And finally, it also has a higher mineral content, including calcium and iron, which are crucial for bone health and preventing anaemia.

Stepping into the ring in the other green corner, we have the mighty traditionalist, Spinach:

- Spinach is richer in iron, magnesium, and folate than Kale. These nutrients are vital for blood health, muscle function, and foetal development.
- It is high in vitamin K, vitamin A, vitamin C and manganese.
- Spinach contains higher amounts than Kale of certain antioxidants that benefit eye health, such as lutein and zeaxanthin.
- It is lower in calories and oxalates than Kale, making it a better option for people with certain kidney issues.

It will be a very close points decision and the good news is, you're the referee. Whatever you decide is the winner, both Kale and Spinach offer a range of awesome health benefits and are very important to your balanced diet. The choice between them or broccoli might come down to specific nutritional needs, personal taste preferences, and how you prepare and eat them.

Adding all of these vegetables into your diet will be the best way to maximise their distinct nutritional benefits. But hey! As far as I am concerned, if you're getting just one of these in your body regularly, you've got your greens covered. Go ahead and hate the other two as much as you or any Ex-President likes.

CHAPTER 10

MEAL PREPPING AND PLANNING

"IN THE KITCHEN, AS IN LIFE, EVERYTHING DEPENDS ON TIMING."

GORDON RAMSAY

What do I need?

Where does it go?

Why do I need it?

When will I use it?

What do I need to make it work?

Organising your shopping, kitchen ingredients and meals properly and efficiently is the kind of logistics operation many of us will appreciate. We do the same type of organising when planning camping or a road trip because it makes sense.

If you're not accustomed to cooking and shopping for yourself, don't worry. Getting your kitchen operating effectively does not need to be difficult. Just follow these steps for your meal prepping and planning, and they will assist your health, save you time and reduce food waste.

Step 1: Get across the nutrition basics

You totally have this covered already. If not, flick back a couple of chapters and review all the prior content of the book. The list of basic foods and ingredients in the prior Chapters is an excellent start to understanding the fundamentals of a balanced healthy diet, which as you know, includes a variety of fruits, vegetables, whole grains, lean proteins and healthy fats. Understanding different foods and their health value will help serve as the foundation for planning your meals and making better-informed choices at the supermarket.

Step 2: Know what you want to cook

Begin with planning meals for a week. The recipes in this book are deliberately developed as a starting point for your meal plans and are not complicated. This planning will help you avoid the temptation of unhealthy convenience foods and will give valuable discipline and structure to your shopping trips.

Step 3: Get a list together

This is easy for you, too. Choose the meals you want from this book (or any other healthy cookbook you might have) and just write down the ingredients you'll need. I have always used the Notes section of my phone for this. Organise your list by supermarket sections (fruit and vegetables, dairy, meats, etc.) to make your shopping trip more efficient. Remember that this is an operation and a new and important part of your life and routine.

Step 4: Shop smart like a boss

When you enter the supermarket, imagine you have limited time to do the shopping. Gamify the whole thing in your mind or do whatever you have to to stick to your list to avoid impulse buys that might not be the healthiest choices. See how fast you can get your shop done. When in the supermarket or grocery store, focus most on the perimeter of the supermarket where fresh produce, meats, and dairy are usually located. Limit the amount of processed foods you buy from the aisles. When selecting items, read labels carefully, watching out for added sugars, salt, and unhealthy fats. Do what I do; just get in, get the stuff on the list, and get out.

Step 5: Think like a chef

When you're done shopping, immediately take some time to prepare meals or some of your meal components before the time of the actual meal. This is what chefs do every day before they serve their customers and it's what I did too. Normally I would shop on a weekend and when I got home, I'd do some preparation like washing, chopping and storing vegetables, marinating some meats or cooking a batch of grains or pasta. Again, this is about having a reliable and healthy routine you can use as part of a new framework for your life. This can save you lots of time during the week and be very satisfying. Your prep activity makes the meal-cooking process less daunting and helps keep you on track to ensure you have readily available components for healthy meals, ready to go.

Step 6: Start cooking up a storm

With your ingredients prepped ahead of time and your recipes at hand, you can start cooking! The recipes in this book are simple and only require basic cooking techniques, such as sautéing, boiling, or baking. If you've never really cooked before, you will see what a therapeutic and rewarding experience it can be and you'll feel a sense of accomplishment.

> *Just repeating this - play music while you prepare meals and cook in the kitchen or listen to podcasts that will keep you motivated and having fun. Get yourself a Bluetooth speaker for this purpose.*

Step 7: Gotta love a leftover

Cooking in bigger batches and embracing the leftovers can be a time and money saver. Many meals you cook can be repurposed in different ways throughout the week, which will reduce your food waste and the need to cook daily. The recipes here are for more than one for that reason. You'll have more for later.

Step 8: Gradually expand your skills

As you become more comfortable in the kitchen and get familiar with the recipes described here or other basic recipes you might find, you can gradually start experimenting with more complex recipes and diverse ingredients. This will enhance your cooking skills and add even more variety to your diet. Email me when you want recipes that move you up a level in the kitchen and I'll write you a whole new book!

Step 9: Enjoy the process

Remember, we are not trying to be five-star chefs here. This is a journey, and it's worth remembering that your persistence is more important than your talent in every area of life. Keep in mind, like all things, cooking is a skill that improves with practice. Just be patient with yourself. Laugh at the burnt things and enjoy the process of learning. This is a valuable opportunity for you to explore new tastes, nurture your body and mind into a much stronger place and perhaps even discover a new passion.

When you are facing the new challenge of cooking for yourself post-divorce or separation, embracing the process of meal planning, shopping and preparation can be incredibly fulfilling. Remember that it's your chance to take control of your health, experiment with new flavours, and find joy in the simple act of nourishing yourself and others. With each meal you prepare, you'll take a step towards a healthier, more independent life and an entirely new and improved version of yourself.

SMART SHOPPING TIPS

- **Learn to read labels:** Pay attention to nutrition labels to make healthier choices. Look for items low in added sugars, sodium and unhealthy fats while rich in fibre, vitamins and minerals.
- **Avoid processed foods:** Sure they're convenient, but processed foods often contain high levels of sodium, sugar and unhealthy fats. If you must buy processed items, opt for the shortest ingredient lists and ingredients you recognise.
- **Buy seasonal produce:** Seasonal fruits and vegetables are often fresher, more flavourful, and less expensive. They also vary your diet throughout the year.
- **Remember those frozen vegetables and fruits:** Frozen produce can be just as nutritious as fresh and is a convenient option to always have on hand, reducing waste from spoilage.
- **Don't shop hungry:** Shopping on an empty stomach can lead to impulse buys of unhealthy foods. Have a snack or meal before you go to avoid this.
- **Get quality proteins:** Look for lean cuts of meat and consider plant-based proteins like beans, lentils, and tofu as nutritious and budget-friendly alternatives.
- **Better bulk buys:** Buying in bulk can save money, especially for non-perishable items like rice, pasta, and canned goods. Just ensure you have the storage space before you get it.

- **Practice portion control:** Buying more than you need can lead to waste. Purchase amounts that you can realistically consume or know will be eaten as leftovers, especially when it comes to perishable items.
- **Stay flexible:** You may need more experience for this tip but sometimes sales or seasonal produce can inspire meal ideas. Flexibility with your meal plan can save money and introduce variety into your diet.
- **Send the kids if you have them:** Why not get the kids to grab certain items for a reward to make your grocery shopping fun for them and even faster for you?

THE DINNER TABLE IS A VITAL INGREDIENT

Before we get into the recipes, I want to let you know about some things I've learned about the profound importance of having meals at the dinner table. I want to make sure you do it. If it is something you have always done like I have, then that's great, keep it up. If it is not, then please add it to your new routine. It's not only incredibly beneficial to you, but if you have kids, it's even more vital, especially in times of stress.

I know that you will often eat alone, and that's ok, but when you have the chance to eat with others, do it at the table. The full scientific references to this are listed at the back of the book.

Here's the proof of the value of a meal together at the table:

Better mental health and wellbeing

Any time you can have a meal with supportive friends or family at the kitchen table, it will increase everyone's feelings of connectedness and belonging. You will also feel their social support more strongly. If you're a dad like me, these regular family meals will literally lower the levels of stress, anxiety and depression, not just for you but if you have adolescent kids, the same will apply to them! (Fulkerson et al., 2006). Any conversations you have here will also give everyone a moment and the time to express themselves, be validated, heard, and bond together. The outcome is enhanced overall emotional well-being for all of you (Eisenberg et al., 2004).

Improved communications skills for kids

If you have young kids or teenagers, your dinner table conversations are extremely powerful for their learning. They assist the development of their communication and interpersonal skills. This is because they encourage active listening, turn-taking, and respectful dialogue. In fact, they literally promote the development of their language, vocabulary and social competence (Rollins et al., 2010). So make sure you have regular meals at the dinner table with your kids, because you will be setting them up as better communicators, with stronger conflict resolution skills (Utter et al., 2018).

A healthy eating routine

Most of the time when you eat with other people at the table, you eat better foods such as fruits, vegetables, and whole grains and fewer unhealthy foods, such as fast food and sugary beverages (Neumark-Sztainer et al., 2003). That's an easy win. For dads, these mealtimes also allow you to model and reinforce healthy eating habits for your kids (Berge et al., 2014). And they'll thank you later for forcing them to eat their veggies now :)

Develop a strong new unit

When you eat at the table with any supportive family members, it's a positive bonding experience. Whether it's with family who are helping you right now, or if it's with your kids, when you eat together you connect, share and strengthen your relationships which helps bring all of you together as a unit (Fiese et al., 2002) and can contribute to the kind of positive family atmosphere you will want to create (De Backer et al., 2015).

Get better learning results

If you have young kids or teenagers, dinner time at the table will help get them better academic results. Your mealtime conversations are a perfect opportunity for their intellectual stimulation, knowledge sharing and cognitive development (Hofferth & Sandberg, 2001). Not only that but your kids will also have higher educational aspirations (Musick & Meier, 2012).

Having dinner at the dinner table is such a simple and normal part of daily life, its huge importance to you, your new routine, your family and your kids if you have them can be overlooked in the stress and turmoil of your separation period. But don't let that happen. Having regular meals at the dinner table is a vital ingredient in your new life and a major part of the recipe for the new you.

Now that you have decided and agreed that you'll eat meals at the dinner table (including breakfast and lunch when you can) you are ready to cook.

Enjoy the process of making the following 30 easy, quick, healthy and delicious meals for your breakfast, lunch and dinner, plus that bonus smoothies section I added because, why not? Remember, I've kept these ideas pretty basic and simple for you. Just follow the method and relax.

Let's move into the kitchen, a foundational ingredient in your new life.

WILL YOU BE THE DIFFERENCE IN SOMEONE ELSE'S LIFE?

"IN THE MIDDLE OF DIFFICULTY LIES OPPORTUNITY."

ALBERT EINSTEIN

Before we get to breakfast, I just wanted to take a quick stop mid-journey to ask you a small but extremely important favour.

As we both know, the path can be pretty dark. We often feel very alone. What I hoped to create in "The Divorced Man's Kitchen Survival Guide" is some kind of light to shine on that path. I shared my story and learnings in the hope of helping others like you.

Will you be happy to do the same?

> I'd be hugely grateful if you'd share your thoughts on this book with other men finding their way through similar challenges.

Did you know that men in the armed services say that the experience of separation and divorce holds more fear and pain than war itself? We all know how tough this is. Your review will be infinitely more than just words, it'll be a powerful signal of hope, a reminder of the strength inside all of us.

You may know someone else on a similar journey. Your recommendation could be a vital ingredient they need. Beyond that, you could help any man - think of anyone's brother, son, uncle, nephew, dad or even grandfather who might need help. Your review could genuinely help him:

- Discover his inner strength and full potential
- Get through the hardest time in his life
- Take better care of himself and his children or loved ones
- Rediscover joy and contentment in life
- Find unexpected love and happiness

What do you think? I'd really appreciate it, and so would plenty of men who neither of us will ever know.

I wrote this book because we needed this. There was no resource I could find anywhere that offered anything like it. This book is a reminder that you and any other man is not alone in their journey and that the greatest strength exists inside them.

To leave your review, just head to Amazon, search this book title and hit 'Create Review'.

Or you can refer to the link below. Your feedback will not only touch the lives of fellow readers but also contribute to a larger narrative of healing and hope for men everywhere:

https://www.amazon.com/review/review-your-purchases/?asin=978-1-7638033-0-5

In sharing, you will join our community of voices. We are all unique but we are also united in the belief that from the ashes of our old lives, we can rise renewed and stronger and better - dare I say, with a Chef's knife in one hand and hope in the other!

Thank you for your support. I'm eternally grateful that you are here and I'm really glad we're on this journey together. Together, let's continue to turn the pages to a new life chapter.

With deepest gratitude,

Christopher H Gillard

CHAPTER 11
IT'S BREAKFAST TIME

"I WENT TO A RESTAURANT THAT SERVES 'BREAKFAST AT ANY TIME'. SO I ORDERED FRENCH TOAST DURING THE RENAISSANCE."

STEVEN WRIGHT

Good morning!

With 10 easy, healthy breakfasts to get you up and going for the day and feeling really good about yourself, your new routine and your new life starts now!

AVOCADO AND EGG TOAST

Tell me what's better than the creaminess of avocado with the richness of a fried egg on toast? This is an easy, fast, delicious and balanced meal you can prepare and eat in about five minutes! Just mash ripe avocado on toasted whole grain bread, top with a poached or fried egg (I use the organic free-range ones), sprinkle with salt, pepper, and chopped parsley and you are done! Give it a go.

Image: This is a pretty good rendition of the dish by AI, however, I'd cook the egg a little more.

Ingredients

1 ripe avocado
2 slices of whole grain bread
2 eggs
Salt, to taste
Freshly ground black pepper, to taste
Fresh parsley, finely chopped
Olive oil or butter (for frying the eggs)

Putting it together

Prepare the Avocado

1. Halve the avocado (be very careful with the knife) and remove the pit. Scoop the flesh into a bowl.

2. Mash the avocado with a fork until you're happy with the texture. Add some salt and pepper to taste.

Toast the Bread

3. While the mashing is happening, toast the whole grain bread slices.

Fry the Eggs

4. Heat a small amount of olive oil or butter in a non-stick or cast iron frying pan over medium heat.
5. Crack the eggs into the pan. For a sunny-side-up egg, let it cook until the whites are set but the yolk is still runny which will take about 2-3 minutes at that heat. Add salt and pepper.

Finish

6. Spread the mashed avocado evenly over the toasted whole-grain bread slices.
7. Carefully place your fried (or whatever way you cooked it) egg on top of each avocado-topped toast.
8. Season with a little more salt and pepper, according to your taste. Chop up some fresh parsley and sprinkle it over the top.

Serve it now

Don't wait! Eat it now while the toast is crunchy, the avocado is creamy and the egg is still warm.

Now you can get on with your day feeling good about yourself.

OVERNIGHT CHIA AND BERRY YOGURT PARFAIT

This recipe is really flexible and you can customise it according to your tastes. For example, different types of milk, flavoured yoghurt, fresh berries or even fruits like passionfruit to create new flavours and textures.

Yes, it looks impressive, but it is so easy for you to make! Check it out.

Image: This is one of the best images AI developed. I think everything about it is pretty spot-on. Well done, my trusty (soon-to-be) Digital Overlord!

Ingredients

1/4 cup chia seeds
1 cup Greek yoghurt (unsweetened)
1 cup almond milk (unsweetened)
1 cup frozen mixed berries
Optional: honey or maple syrup for sweetness, to taste (I prefer maple)
Optional for garnish: granola, nuts, or additional fresh berries

Putting it together

Mix the Chia Pudding

1. In a medium bowl, whisk together the chia seeds, almond milk, and 1/2 cup of your Greek yoghurt. If you prefer a sweeter taste (like I do), add maple syrup or honey at this point.

2. Let it sit for about 5 minutes, then stir again to break up any clumps of chia seeds.
3. Cover the bowl and refrigerate it overnight. While you sleep, the chia seeds will absorb the liquid and expand like a football team in a pub.

Prepare the Berries

4. I like lightly mashing the slightly defrosted berries with a fork for a more "compote-like" texture. I also mix them with a bit of maple syrup and refrigerate them overnight with the chia pudding mix.

Putting the Parfait Together

5. In the morning, check the consistency of the chia. If it's extra gluey and pretty thick, you can adjust it by stirring in a little more almond milk until you reach your desired consistency.
6. Take a glass or jar and start layering your parfait. Begin with a layer of the chia pudding, followed by a layer of Greek yoghurt, and then a layer of the prepared mixed berries.
7. Repeat the layers until the glass or jar is filled.
8. Top the parfait with the remaining Greek yoghurt and a final layer of berries.

Garnish and Serve

For added texture and flavour, garnish your parfait with granola, nuts, or additional fresh berries if you have them.

Now get it into you!

WARM OATS WITH ALMOND AND BERRY

This porridge is admittedly, slightly up itself, but not to the level of being wildly pretentious. Really it's just warm oats with a quick makeover. This is your nice, quick, comfort food for any morning, but especially Winter. And is there a better start to your day (especially a cold one) than creamy oatmeal, tart berries, rich yoghurt, crunchy almonds and sweet maple syrup?

Image: The berries in this AI image look appealing and the oats appear perfectly cooked, with the right amount of moisture, but I'd personally add crushed, toasted almonds on the top, rather than whole raw ones.

Ingredients

1 cup rolled oats
2 cups almond milk
1 cup mixed frozen berries
Greek yoghurt for serving
Slivered almonds for garnish
Maple syrup for drizzling
Cinnamon powder
Vanilla extract

Putting it together

Cook the Oatmeal

1. In a medium saucepan, combine the rolled oats and almond milk. I also add a pinch of cinnamon and vanilla extract for extra flavour punch but you can leave them out if you prefer.
2. Bring the mixture to a boil over medium heat, then reduce the heat to low.
3. Simmer for 5-7 minutes, stirring occasionally, until the oats are soft and the porridge has thickened to your liking.

Warm the Berries

4. While the oatmeal is cooking, place the mixed frozen berries in a small saucepan over low heat and a little splash of water. Warm them gently, just until they're defrosted and release their juices, creating what's called a berry "compote". A faster method is to microwave the berries in a microwave-safe bowl for 1-2 minutes or until warm.

Serve the Porridge

5. Spoon the warm oatmeal porridge into serving bowls.

Top each bowl with a generous spoonful of the warm mixed berry compote. Add a dollop of Greek yoghurt to each serving.

Make it Prettier and Eat it

Sprinkle slivered almonds over the top. Drizzle with maple syrup. Serve up and eat fast before Goldilocks arrives.

This recipe is easy to make and highly customisable. You can use honey, rice syrup or maple syrup for flavour and different toppings depending on what you have on hand.

BANANA AND RICOTTA HONEY RICE CAKES

This recipe is incredibly versatile, allowing for various substitutions based on your own dietary needs or preferences. For example, a dairy-free version could use almond or coconut-based ricotta cheese. Additionally, you can experiment with different toppings like berries, sliced peaches, or a sprinkle of cocoa powder to customise even more. And as you have already heard me say before, you can use maple syrup instead of honey or blend the bananas and honey into the ricotta mix to create a puree.

Image: This is so easy it's almost an overstatement to call it a recipe.
It's a fast, healthy and light breakfast and it tastes great.

Ingredients

2 rice cakes
1/2 cup ricotta cheese
1 ripe banana
2 tablespoons honey, plus more for drizzling
A pinch of cinnamon (optional)
A handful of crushed nuts or seeds (such as almonds, walnuts, or chia seeds) for garnish

Putting it together

Prepare the Ricotta Blend

1. In a small bowl, blend the ricotta cheese with 1 tablespoon of honey until smooth. If you have a blender or food processor, you can use it for a smoother consistency. Add a pinch of cinnamon for a hint of warmth and spice.

Slice the Banana

2. Peel and thinly slice the banana. Set aside a few slices for topping.

Assemble the Rice Cakes

3. Spread a generous layer of the sweetened ricotta mixture over each rice cake.
4. Arrange the banana slices on top of the ricotta.

Add Toppings

5. Drizzle the remaining honey over the banana slices. The honey adds sweetness and helps keep the banana slices in place. That's clever engineering right there.
6. Sprinkle it with crushed nuts or seeds for added texture and a nutritional boost.

Consume Immediately

Enjoy your Blended Banana and Ricotta Honey Rice Cakes right now for the best texture and flavour.

Could this be any simpler? Spread ricotta cheese mix over rice cakes and top with sliced bananas and honey for a quick and tasty breakfast. Almost zero effort.

TUNA AND AVOCADO ON TOASTED DARK RYE BREAD

I love tinned tuna and this breakfast is so simple and fast to make. It's a great meal to eat a couple of hours before your workout too. The combination of creamy avocado, savoury tuna, and the full flavour of dark rye bread, garnished with black pepper and red onion, creates an incredibly satisfying meal for any time of day.

Image: Again, this is a good visual approximation of the dish by AI, but the onion should be finely diced.

Ingredients

2 slices of dark rye bread
1 ripe avocado
1 can of tuna in olive oil
Freshly ground black pepper, to taste
1 small red onion, finely sliced
Optional: lemon juice, to taste
Optional: extra virgin olive oil, for drizzling
Optional: fresh herbs (such as parsley or cilantro) for garnish

Putting it together

Toast the Bread

Toast the slices of dark rye bread to your desired level of crispiness.

Prepare the Avocado

1. Halve the avocado, remove the pit, and scoop the flesh into a bowl.
2. Mash the avocado with a fork until you like the look and texture of it. For a bit of zest, I like to add a few drops of lemon juice and a pinch of salt to the avocado mix.

Make the Tuna Mix

3. In a separate bowl, break up the drained tuna and mix it through the oil from the tin. Add salt to taste.

Spread Avocado on Toast

4. Spread the mashed avocado evenly over the toasted dark rye bread slices.

Add the Tuna

5. Place the tuna mix on top of the mashed avocado.

Garnish

6. Season with freshly ground black pepper to taste. Add the finely sliced red onion on top of the tuna. I love the onion's sharpness and how it complements the creamy avocado and savoury flavour of the tuna. If you like, drizzle a little extra virgin olive oil over the top for richness and garnish with fresh herbs for added flavour and a pop of colour.

Serve it up

Enjoy your Tuna and Avocado on Toasted Dark Rye Bread immediately for the best combination of textures and flavours.

There you have it — a balanced and nutritious breakfast that's fast to prepare, delicious and incredibly versatile. It can be adapted using tinned salmon or sardines instead of tuna for example, or you might prefer the texture and flavour of multigrain bread, along with diced pickled onions, rather than fresh ones. No excuses not to give it a go!

EGG AND CHORIZO BREAKFAST BURRITO

How do you do it? Simple!

Just sauté chorizo sausage and mix through your scrambled eggs. Place all that on a warm whole grain tortilla, add your diced tomatoes and basil on top of that and wrap the whole thing up for a spicy kick start to your day!

Image: I'll admit, AI did have a good go at this dish, however, it overcooked the egg to a rubbery consistency even though the recipe clearly describes how to avoid this. Unlike AI, make sure you cook your scrambled eggs, GENTLY.

Ingredients

2 whole grain tortillas
4 large free range eggs
100g chorizo, diced
1 medium tomato, diced
Fresh basil leaves, for garnish
Smoked paprika, for flavour and garnish
Salt and pepper, to taste
Olive oil, for cooking

Putting it together

Cook the Chorizo

1. Heat a non-stick pan over medium heat. When it's hot, add a drizzle of olive oil and the diced chorizo. Cook for 2-3 minutes, or until the chorizo is slightly crispy and releases its oils.

Scramble the Eggs

2. In a bowl, beat the eggs with some salt and pepper and a pinch of smoked paprika.
3. Pour the eggs into the pan with the chorizo. Let the eggs sit briefly before gently stirring the whole lot until the eggs form soft curds.
4. Remove the pan from the heat and the eggs will still cook due to the contained heat. This way they will remain light and fluffy and you won't get a rubbery texture with liquid oozing out of them which happens when you cook scrambled eggs at too high a temperature.

Warm the Tortillas

5. Warm the whole grain tortillas in a separate clean pan or directly over the flame of a gas stove for a few seconds on each side, just until they're flexible and slightly toasted.

Assemble your Dish

6. Place the warm tortillas on plates. Spoon the scrambled egg and chorizo mixture evenly onto each tortilla.
7. Fold the tortillas over the filling then top with the diced fresh tomatoes and a sprinkle of smoked paprika for added colour and flavour. Optionally, add a drizzle of olive oil or a hot sauce like Tabasco for extra zest.

Garnish and Serve

Tip: Want to customise this recipe a bit? No worries. Add cheese or avocado or swap the chorizo for another protein like bacon or ham.

It's virtually impossible <u>not</u> to enjoy this one and it's an excellent way to start your day :)

BANANA AND MANGO TROPICAL SMOOTHIE

Why not hit the tropics this morning after your run or workout? This delicious, healthy smoothie is fast to make and even more potent with the addition of hemp powder, which will give you a serious protein boost.

Image: In the wildly romantic world inhabited by AI, this is an image from a secluded balcony in Tahiti. There's also pirates treasure buried under that palm tree.

Ingredients

1 ripe banana, peeled and sliced
1 cup frozen mango chunks
1 cup coconut milk (can use light coconut milk for a lower-fat option)
2 tablespoons hemp protein powder
Optional: 1 tablespoon honey or maple syrup
Optional: Ice cubes for a colder smoothie (a good idea in Summer)
Optional garnish: A sprinkle of spirulina, a few slices of banana or mango, or a sprinkle of shredded coconut

Putting it together

Blend the Smoothie

1. In a blender, combine the sliced banana, frozen mango chunks, coconut milk and hemp protein powder. If you prefer a sweeter smoothie, add honey or maple syrup to taste. For a colder smoothie in Summer, add a few ice cubes.

Blend Until Smooth

2. Blend on high speed until all the ingredients are thoroughly combined and the smoothie is smooth and creamy. If it's too thick you can add a little more coconut milk to reach your desired consistency.

Serve

3. Pour the smoothie into a glass or bowl.
If you want it to look a bit fancy, add banana or mango slices, or some shredded coconut on top.

Enjoy

Don't wait - drink it now!

The protein from hemp powder and the healthy fats from coconut milk combined with the properties of the banana, make this a perfect post-workout recovery drink as well as a great tasting breakfast.

FARMHOUSE TOASTIE

This is my more exciting version of the traditional tomato and cheese toastie and it only requires you to add a couple of extra cheeses. It's a highly addictive combo of tomato and parsley, creamy ricotta, the tang of goat's cheese, and the sharpness of vintage cheddar. Sometimes you need to indulge.

Image: AI cut the tomato slices way too thick and the cheese is not melted enough. These are unacceptable, basic errors by a thing that apparently knows everything. My girls would be very unimpressed. But looking at the positives, that country morning vibe is awesome.

Ingredients

2 slices of your preferred bread (sourdough or whole grain works well for the texture and flavour)
1/2 cup of diced fresh tomato
1/4 cup of goat cheese, crumbled
A slice or 1/4 cup of grated vintage cheddar cheese
1/4 cup of ricotta cheese
A small handful of fresh parsley, chopped
Salt and pepper, to taste
Olive oil or butter, for toasting

Putting it together

Prep the Filling

1. In a bowl, combine the diced fresh tomato, crumbled goats cheese, grated vintage cheddar, ricotta cheese, and chopped parsley. Season the mixture with salt and pepper to taste.
2. Gently mix to distribute the ingredients evenly.

Add Filling to Bread

3. Lay out the slices of bread on your cutting board. Spread the cheese and tomato mixture evenly over one slice of bread (right to the edges).
4. Place the second slice of bread on top. Hey look, a sandwich!

Toast it

5. Heat a non-stick pan or sandwich press to medium heat. If it's a pan, brush the outside of the sandwich lightly with olive oil or butter for a golden crust.
6. Place the sandwich in the pan or sandwich press. Cook for about 3-4 minutes on each side, pressing down lightly with your spatula if using a pan, until the bread is toasted to a golden brown and the cheeses have melted.

Serve

7. Once toasted, remove it from the pan, it cool for a minute and slice it in half or quarters. Eat it ASAP while the cheese is warm and gooey and the bread is crispy.

Now try telling me this isn't extremely satisfying. That's right. You can't.

ONE PAN SPANISH EGGS AND BEANS

This dish is all about the mix of textures and flavours. You've got the spicy and meaty chorizo with the creamy baked beans and soft, rich eggs, all balanced by the cool, crisp cucumber. This is great fuel for your day, and it's all done in one pan. You and your tastebuds enjoy that trip to Barcelona!

Image: AI goes to the fresh food market in Barcelona, exactly as asked, but doesn't combine the ingredients enough and undercooks the egg for me! Man! What is it with AI and eggs?

Ingredients

1 tablespoon olive oil
100g (about 3.5 oz) chorizo sausage, diced
1 small red onion, diced
4 large free-range eggs
1 can (about 400g or 14 oz) baked beans
Salt and black pepper, to taste
1 teaspoon dried basil
A pinch of chilli flakes (adjust to taste)
1 small cucumber, thinly sliced

Putting it together

Cook the Chorizo and Onion

1. Heat the olive oil in a large pan over medium heat.
2. Add the diced chorizo and cook for about 2-3 minutes until it starts to release its oils.
3. Add the diced red onion to the pan and sauté with the chorizo until the onion is soft and translucent, which will be about 5 minutes.

Add the Baked Beans

4. Pour the can of baked beans into the pan with the chorizo and onion. Stir to combine and let the mixture heat for a few minutes.

Season the Mixture

5. Season the mixture with salt, black pepper, dried basil, and chilli flakes. Stir well to make sure your seasonings are evenly distributed.

Crack in the Eggs

6. Make four wells in the mixture with the back of a spoon. Crack an egg into each well. Season the eggs with a little more salt and pepper.

Cover and Cook

7. Reduce the heat to low, cover the pan with a lid, and let the eggs cook to your desired level. (For runny yolks, cook for about 4-6 minutes or for firmer yolks, cook for 7-9 minutes).

Garnish and Serve

8. Once the eggs are cooked the way you like them, remove the pan from the heat. Garnish the top of the dish with thinly sliced cucumber, which is a really great, crispy fresh contrast to the heartiness of the beans and chorizo.

I usually just eat this straight from the pan and there's no reason you can't either!

BIRCHER MUESLI WITH FRESH KIWI FRUIT

I totally love Bircher Muesli. It's a wholesome and refreshing breakfast option you can easily prepare the night before and it was invented by a Swiss doctor over 120 years ago, so it has to be the healthiest thing ever. It combines the natural sweetness and textures of fruits with the creaminess of Greek yoghurt.

Image: AI gets the bullseye for the nostalgic, fairytale feel of the Swiss Alps, but can't help piling on ridiculous amounts of Kiwi Fruit. Why?

Ingredients

1 cup rolled oats
1 large apple, grated (with skin for extra fibre)
1 cup orange juice (freshly squeezed for the best flavour)
2 tablespoons honey (more or less, according to your taste)
1/2 teaspoon ground cinnamon
1/2 cup Greek yoghurt (plus more for serving)
1-2 kiwi fruits, peeled and sliced

Putting it together

Soak the Oats

1. In a large mixing bowl, combine the rolled oats and orange juice. Ensure the oats are fully submerged in the juice. This soaking process will soften the oats and infuse them with the orange flavour.

Mix in Apple and Flavourings

2. Add the grated apple to the soaked oats. The apple adds great texture and natural sweetness.
3. Stir in the honey and ground cinnamon, adjusting the quantities to suit your taste. These two ingredients will give your Bircher Muesli even more depth of flavour.

Add your Greek Yoghurt

4. Fold in the Greek yoghurt until it's well combined. The yoghurt adds a creamy texture and a tangy contrast to the sweetness of the fruit and honey.

Chill

5. Cover the bowl with a lid or plastic wrap and put it in the fridge overnight. This allows the flavours to combine and the oats to become tender.

Serve with Kiwi

6. When you're about to serve, first give the muesli a good stir. If it's too thick, you can loosen it up with a little more orange juice or Greek yoghurt. Spoon your fresh Bircher Muesli into a bowl and top with the sliced kiwi fruit. The kiwi adds bright colour, tangy flavour and another big boost of vitamin C.

Enjoy

Eat it and enjoy the fact that you've made something delicious and perfectly good for you. This stuff can keep you going all day too.

You can add other fruits, nuts, and seeds according to your preferences or whatever you have in the kitchen. Except meat. (I hope you already knew that).

CHAPTER 12
LUNCHTIME

"DESTINY MAY RIDE WITH US TODAY, BUT THERE IS NO REASON FOR IT TO INTERFERE WITH LUNCH."

PETER THE GREAT

All the best people stop for lunch, and you should too.

Often, lunch recipes can easily translate into dinner meals, which is a positive thing. So bear in mind that the following lunch recipes are not time-limited for your consumption in the middle of the day and you will find a few ideas you might want to make as the evening meal. They're also straightforward in terms of the preparation and perfect for taking to work or eating at home.

SOUTHERN ROAST CHICKEN AND AVOCADO WRAP

Wraps are great for lunch, and anyone can make one. With cold roast chicken, mashed avocado, cheddar cheese and refried beans, this wrap is extra tasty, satisfying, portable and simple.

Image: No matter how many times I asked it, AI would not combine the wrap ingredients, it kept them separated for some reason. It happened so much, I even began to suspect it was doing it on purpose. Anyway, I'd mix it up a bit more and cut the chicken slightly smaller.

Ingredients

1 large wholegrain wrap
1/2 cup cold roast chicken, shredded or diced
One half of a ripe avocado
1/2 cup refried beans (canned or homemade)
1/2 cup of grated cheddar cheese
chilli powder, to taste
Cracked black pepper, to taste
Salt, to taste

Putting it together

Prepare the Avocado

1. Cut the avocado in half, remove the pit, and use a spoon to scoop out the flesh of one half into a bowl.

2. Mash it up with a fork until you like how it looks.
Season the mashed avocado with a pinch of salt, chilli powder, and black pepper to taste. Mix it up well.

Warm the Wrap

3. Heat the wholegrain wrap in a dry pan over medium heat for about 30 seconds on each side, just until warm and pliable. Alternatively, you can microwave it for 10-15 seconds.

Make your Wrap

4. Place the warm wholegrain wrap flat on a plate or cutting board.
5. Spread the refried beans evenly over the wrap's surface, leaving a small border around the edges.
6. Scoop the mashed avocado over the top of the refried beans.
7. Spread grated cheddar cheese on top of the avocado and distribute the cold roast chicken pieces over everything else.

Season

8. Sprinkle some more chilli powder, cracked black pepper and a pinch of salt over the chicken, according to your taste preferences.

Wrap It Up

9. Carefully fold the sides of the wrap towards the centre and then roll it up from the bottom to enclose the filling securely.

Eat it

You are very hungry by now, so just cut the wrap in half and eat that thing.

There are days when roast chicken and avocado with the heartiness of refried beans, all packaged up in a wholesome wholegrain wrap is just what you're after. The hint of chilli powder gives this some satisfying punch too, for those (like me) who like a little heat.

BLACK BEAN, CORN AND GOAT CHEESE QUESADILLA

While we are in the 'wraps' zone, here's another recipe inspired by Mexican and Spanish cuisines, which (you may have noticed) I happen to love for their health and flavour benefits.

This is a fast and delicious combo of the sweetness of corn with the richness of black beans and goat cheese, enveloped in a crispy whole-grain tortilla.

Image: You'd think asking AI to write 'roadhouse' instead of 'road-house' would be simple but you'd be wrong. It would be easier to thread a needle on a rollercoaster. Not only that, but again, it used way too much of something (goats cheese) and refused to mash the beans or add the coriander. What the hell? At least YOU can follow the recipe.

Ingredients

2 whole grain tortillas
1 cup canned black beans, rinsed and drained
1/2 cup creamed corn (canned or homemade)
1 teaspoon smoked paprika
1/2 cup goat cheese, crumbled
A small handful of washed, chopped fresh coriander (cilantro)
Salt and pepper, to taste
Olive oil for the pan

Putting it together

Prepare the Filling

1. In a bowl, lightly mash the black beans with a fork. You're aiming for a partially mashed texture with some whole beans remaining. Just use your judgement.
2. Add the smoked paprika to the beans, season with salt and pepper, and mix well to combine it all.

Assemble the Quesadillas

3. Lay one whole-grain tortilla flat on your cutting board. Spread half of the bean mixture over the tortilla, leaving a small border around the edges (this is to prevent spillage).
4. Spoon the creamed corn evenly over the bean layer.
5. Sprinkle the crumbled goat cheese and chopped coriander over the top.
6. Cover with the second tortilla.

Cook the Quesadilla

7. Heat a large non-stick pan over medium heat, and once it is hot, lightly coat it with olive oil.
8. Immediately (carefully) place the assembled quesadilla in the pan. Cook for 2-3 minutes or until the bottom tortilla is golden and crispy.
9. Now carefully flip the quesadilla and cook for another 2-3 minutes on the other side until crispy and the cheese has melted.

Eat that thing

10. Remove the quesadilla from the pan and let it cool for a minute if you can handle the suspense, before cutting into wedges. Serve it hot. You can add sides like salsa, sour cream, jalapeños and extra chopped coriander. (I would add everything).

If you can't get to a roadhouse in Texas by lunchtime, then just make the "Black Bean, Corn, and Goat Cheese Quesadilla" and imagine the roadhouse (with no hyphen) instead.

GOLDEN FRIED TOFU AND AVOCADO RICE BOWL

Want to add a Japanese feel to your lunch day? This delicious and nutritious dish combines the rich flavours of marinated tofu with the creaminess of avocado and the wholesomeness of brown rice. Keep going, and find out how to prepare this extremely satisfying meal.

Image: No-one wants their tofu that big and chunky but other than that, this is a pretty good job by AI. (It's a glass of green tea and a small dish of sweet soy in the background which is a nice touch).

Ingredients

1 cup brown rice
2 cups water (for cooking the rice)
400g (approx. 14 oz) firm tofu, cubed
2 tablespoons soy sauce (for marinating)
1 tablespoon sesame oil (for marinating)
1 tablespoon sweet chilli sauce (for marinating)
1 ripe avocado, sliced
Sesame seeds, for garnish
Sweet soy sauce, for drizzling
Olive oil or another vegetable oil, for frying

Putting it together

Cook the Rice

Rinse the brown rice under cold water until the water runs clear.

In a pot, combine the rinsed rice and water. Bring to a boil, then reduce the heat to low, cover, and simmer for about 45 minutes, or until the rice is tender and the water is absorbed.

Remove from heat and let it sit, covered, for 5 minutes before fluffing with a fork.

Marinate the Tofu

In a bowl, mix the soy sauce, sesame oil, and sweet chilli sauce.

Add the cubed tofu to the marinade, gently tossing to ensure all pieces are coated. Let it marinate for at least 30 minutes, or for a better flavour, marinate it overnight in the refrigerator.

Fry the Tofu

Heat a large pan or wok over medium-high heat and add a generous amount of olive oil.

Once the oil is hot, add the marinated tofu cubes. Fry until all sides are golden brown and crispy. Remove from the pan and set aside on paper towels to drain any excess oil.

Assemble the Bowl

Scoop a serving of the cooked brown rice into each bowl.

Top the rice with the golden fried tofu cubes and slices of ripe avocado.

Sprinkle sesame seeds over the bowl for a nutty flavour and a crunchy texture.

Serve

Just before serving, drizzle sweet soy sauce over the bowl for an extra layer of flavour. Serve it immediately while the tofu is still warm and the avocado flesh is nice and green. Add a few pieces of pickled ginger on top if you have some, and you'll thank me for it.

This dish is full of flavour, visually appealing and extremely nutritious, with a balance of protein, healthy fats and complex carbohydrates. I bet it's something you'll keep making repeatedly.

QUICK DIVERSION ON TOFU

Image: A block of firm Tofu looks like something you could use on a building site or in tyre construction and many people say it also tastes that way. But if you know how, it can be turned into something a lot more appealing. Stay with me and find out.

Given the unfair reputation Tofu has got itself with some people, I thought I'd add a few tips to help with your preparation. A lot of the problem is that people get frustrated that their Tofu doesn't take on the flavours of their marinade or dish in the way they expect. The reason for this is that there are specific steps you need to take to add to the ability of Tofu to absorb flavours. For some reason, many chefs and lots of recipes, don't describe them.

So I will.

Freeze it first: Freezing tofu first before marinating and cooking it can significantly enhance its ability to take on flavours from your marinade. That's because structural changes occur in the tofu when it is frozen and then thawed. When it freezes, the water content in the tofu forms ice crystals. The ice then expands, creating larger pores and channels within the structure of the tofu.

When you thaw the tofu, the ice melts, but you still have these handy little holes all through it. This new porous structure gives a spongy quality to the tofu, meaning it can absorb more of the marinade and any other flavours than it would in its original firm, dense state.

Press the Tofu: Before you cut and marinate your tofu, it's crucial to press it to remove the excess water. To do this, wrap the tofu block in paper towels or a clean tea towel and place any relatively heavy object (like a heavy pan or a few canned goods) on top of it for about 15 to 30 minutes. When you remove the water you create more 'space' for the marinade to penetrate.

Increase surface area: When you cut the tofu into small pieces, such as cubes, slices, or triangles the added surface area means the marinade has a bigger area to cover, helping your flavour absorption.

Score the Tofu: Scoring is slicing the surface of a thing, usually in a crisscross pattern. You can gently score the tofu's surface with a knife, creating more nooks and crannies for the marinade to seep into, enhancing flavour absorption.

Make sure your marinade is delicious: A good marinade will take your dish to the next level. When putting it together, make sure you get the flavour balance right. I usually go for a mix of sweet and sour ingredients, with a little saltiness in amongst it all. Acid-based elements (like vinegar or citrus juices) can help your tofu absorb flavours more effectively as they help break down the proteins. Any oil you add to the marinade helps to carry fat-soluble flavours into the tofu and seasonings, like chilli, pepper and salt, adds the final punch you are looking for.

Give the marinade time to work: Depending on the strength of your marinade, you will normally need at least 30 minutes for any real absorption to take place. I usually allow several hours, or often overnight in the fridge to enhance flavour absorption. The longer you marinate your tofu, the more flavour it will absorb.

Make it agitated: This doesn't mean you have to annoy your tofu constantly with terrible dad jokes. 'Agitating' in this case is gently turning or stirring the pieces of tofu at times during the marination process so all pieces are evenly exposed and covered in the marinade.

Heat it up: Some flavours will absorb better into tofu when you apply a little heat. Very slowly baking it or gently simmering tofu in the marinade for a small portion of the marination time (at the beginning) can break it down a little and help the flavours penetrate more deeply.

Sorry no official certificate, but now you're a marinated tofu expert. Use your knowledge :)

LEMON CHICKEN AND QUINOA SALAD

If you're doing the workouts and exercise routine, this is a great one for your energy and protein. It's light, but it's a satisfying and healthy lunch. I love the tanginess of this lemon-grilled chicken with the wholesomeness of quinoa and the freshness of cucumber and parsley. The zesty lemon-thyme dressing caps the whole thing off beautifully.

Image: This image is pretty accurate. But just combine all the ingredients a bit more than AI did and cut the chicken into small dice, not lengthways.

Ingredients

2 chicken breasts
2 tablespoons olive oil (plus extra for grilling)
Juice of 1 lemon (plus extra for dressing)
1 cup quinoa
1/4 cup chopped parsley
1 cucumber, diced
1/2 cup crumbled Danish feta
Salt, to taste
1 teaspoon dried thyme

Putting it together

Prepare the Chicken

1. Marinate the chicken breasts with one tablespoon olive oil, the juice of half a lemon, and a pinch of salt. Let it sit for at least 15 minutes (or even overnight if you are well prepared).

2. Heat a grill pan (sometimes called a griddle) over medium-high heat, and when it's hot, grill the chicken until it's cooked through. Let it sit there. You want nice grill marks, about 6-7 minutes per side, depending on the thickness of the breast.

3. Once cooked, let it rest for a few minutes before dicing it into bite-sized pieces. If it's pink in the middle, throw the diced bits back on the grill until the pink goes and they firm up.

Cook the Quinoa

(You can do this ahead of time or while you wait for the marinade to do its thing.)

4. Rinse the quinoa under cold water and drain.

In a medium saucepan, combine the quinoa with 2 cups of water and a pinch of salt.

5. Bring to a boil, then reduce the heat to low, cover, and simmer for about 15 minutes or until all the water is absorbed.

6. Remove from heat and let it sit covered for 5 minutes. Then fluff with a fork and let it cool. If you did it earlier, reheat it in the microwave when needed.

Make the Dressing

7. In a small bowl, whisk together two tablespoons of olive oil, the juice of the remaining half lemon, dried thyme, and salt to taste.

Make the Salad

8. In a large mixing bowl, combine the cooked quinoa, diced chicken, chopped parsley, and small diced cucumber.
9. Pour the lemon-thyme dressing over the salad and toss until everything is well coated.
10. Gently fold in the crumbled Danish feta.

Eat that delicious dish

Get into it. You won't want to wait. You can adjust the seasoning with more salt or lemon juice if needed.

This is always delicious and the kind of thing you can keep in the fridge and eat at any time *if you have leftovers*. If you have them. (Doubtful).

CLASSIC CURRIED EGG SANDWICH

Ever had these? We had them a lot when I was a kid, and they are still a fabulous lunch, now that I am a much older kid. This classic sandwich mixes the smooth texture of curried eggs with the crunch of celery and the malty flavour and chewy texture of dark rye bread to quietly blow your mind.

Image: How's the authenticity of that 1970's tablecloth? AI definitely got the 70's vibe right, but who the heck will eat large chunks of celery like that? No-one, that's who. So make sure you dice it finely and mix it through the egg.

Ingredients

4 medium-boiled eggs, peeled and coarsely chopped
2 tablespoons whole egg mayonnaise
1 teaspoon mild mustard
1/2 to 1 teaspoon curry powder (adjust to your taste)
Salt and pepper, to taste
1/4 cup finely chopped celery
Flattened Iceberg or Cos lettuce leaves
Dark rye bread slices
White vinegar

Boiling the eggs

If you have ever said "I couldn't even boil an egg," well now is your chance to review that statement.

1. First - make sure your eggs are room temperature, or they will immediately crack in the water.
2. Now get a saucepan and fill it with just boiled water from the kettle. Add a few pinches of salt to the water and a large tablespoon of white vinegar (coagulates any white leaching out of a crack). Crank the heat underneath it.
3. When the water is boiling, gently place your eggs into the bottom of the saucepan using a ladle. When the ladle hits the bottom of the pan, slide the egg out slowly so it doesn't crack. Do that for another three eggs.
4. Set your phone timer for about 7 minutes. DO THAT NOW.
5. When your timer goes off, take the saucepan and tip the water and medium boiled eggs into a colander in the sink.
6. Immediately put the eggs into a bowl of ice water or run them under the cold tap. PEEL THEM IMMEDIATELY. Cooling them down fast at this point will make the internal membrane that sits between the egg white and the shell seize up, retract and attach to the shell, rather than the egg white, so peeling them will be simple and fast. If you don't do this, you'll rip chunks of egg white out as you attempt to pull the shell off, which can be a very frustrating experience!
7. Cool them in the fridge.

Now you CAN boil an egg.

Putting it together

Prepare the Curried Egg Mixture

8. In a medium bowl, combine the chopped boiled eggs with mayonnaise, mild mustard and curry powder. Gently stir to mix well.
9. Add the finely chopped celery to the mixture and fold it in for that added crunch. Season with salt and pepper according to your taste preferences.

Make the Sandwich

10. Lay out slices of dark rye bread on your cutting board.
Place flattened lettuce leaves on half of the bread slices. The lettuce adds a fresh crunch and cleverly prevents the bread from becoming soggy.

11. Spoon the curried egg mixture evenly over the lettuce-covered slices. Top with another slice of dark rye bread to complete each sandwich.

Eat it

Cut it in half or quarters if you can be bothered. Actually go on — just eat it whole, we're not judging here.

Medium-boiled eggs with mild mustard, whole egg mayonnaise, curry powder, chopped celery, lettuce and seasoning served on dark rye bread is easy and delicious. Anyone who doesn't agree needs to be viewed with great suspicion and is either a psychopath or a five year old.

MEDITERRANEAN PASTA SALAD

This salad is like a big colourful, loud Greek beach party that some wholesome Italians decided to join. It's always going to be a joyous occasion when you put olive oil, diced cucumber, diced semi-dried tomatoes, diced fresh tomatoes, sliced olives, crumbled Greek feta, lemon juice, oregano and fresh basil together with balsamic vinegar, whole-grain pasta and sea salt.

Image: Everything in the salad is too big and chunky in this AI image and the sea is actually entering the village buildings in the background, which is terrible for the locals. Still, this looks like a pleasant place to eat.

Ingredients

2 cups whole grain pasta such as penne, fusilli, or farfalle
2 tablespoons olive oil
1/2 cup small diced cucumber
2 tablespoons balsamic vinegar
1/2 cup diced semi-dried tomatoes
1/2 cup small diced fresh tomatoes
1/2 cup sliced black olives
1/2 cup crumbled Greek feta cheese
Juice of 1 lemon
1 teaspoon dried oregano
A handful of fresh basil leaves, torn up
Salt and pepper, to taste

Putting it together

Cook the Pasta

1. Bring a large pot of salted water to a boil. Add the whole grain pasta and cook according to package instructions (usually between 8 and 11 minutes) until al dente.

2. Drain and immediately drizzle the pasta with a bit of olive oil to prevent sticking. Toss in some salt and mix it around. Tip: if you want your salad to be cool, put the pasta in the fridge in a container; otherwise keep it handy on your bench where it will stay warm.

Prepare the Dressing While the Pasta Cooks

In a small mixing bowl, whisk together olive oil, balsamic vinegar, lemon juice, oregano, salt, and pepper. Adjust the seasoning according to your taste.

Combine it All

2. In a large mixing bowl, combine the cooked pasta, diced cucumber, semi-dried tomatoes, fresh tomatoes and sliced black olives.

3. Pour the dressing over the pasta mixture and toss well to ensure all the ingredients are evenly coated.

Add Cheese and Herbs

4. Gently fold in the crumbled Greek feta cheese and fresh basil leaves into the salad. The feta adds a creamy tang and the basil provides its fresh, aromatic flavour.

Get Into it

Taste and adjust the seasoning if necessary. The salad can be served immediately or chilled in the refrigerator for an hour or more to allow the flavours to meld together. Before serving, gently toss the salad to redistribute the dressing and ingredients.

You might not be able to sit and relax on an old pier at a Greek fishing village today, but you can still enjoy this Mediterranean Pasta Salad while you let your mind wander.

PROSCIUTTO AND MELON SALAD

Since we have just been to Greece, we might as well head across to Italy, where we will combine slices of prosciutto with little balls of honeydew melon or rockmelon (called Cantaloupe in some places), mint leaves and crumbled Danish feta before we drizzle it all with the sweet addictive tang of balsamic reduction.

Image: Don't be like AI and leave the skin on the melon, ok? Nobody does that. And rip your prosciutto up a lot more. Also the whole thing looks a bit dry, so add more balsamic glaze.

Ingredients

100g (about 3.5 oz) Prosciutto, thinly sliced
1 Honeydew melon or Rockmelon, cut into bite-sized pieces
2 tablespoons olive oil
1 tablespoon honey
100g (about 3.5 oz) Bocconcini, halved or whole depending on size
Balsamic vinegar glaze, for drizzling
A handful of rocket lettuce (Arugula)
A few mint leaves, torn
Fresh basil leaves, torn, to taste
Salt and freshly ground pepper, to taste

Putting it together

Prepare the Melon

1. Using a melon baller or a knife, cut the Honeydew or Cantaloupe into bite-sized pieces or balls. Set aside in your large mixing bowl.

Dress the Melon

2. In a small bowl, whisk the olive oil and honey until well combined. Drizzle this dressing over the melon pieces and gently toss it to coat it evenly.

Make the Salad

3. On a large platter or individual plates, lay out a bed of rocket lettuce.
4. Arrange the dressed melon pieces over the rocket.
5. Drape the prosciutto slices around and over the melon like a true artiste.
6. Scatter the bocconcini pieces throughout the salad.

Garnish

7. Drizzle the balsamic vinegar glaze over the salad to give it that awesome, rich, tangy finish. Don't skimp.
8. Sprinkle torn mint leaves and fresh basil over the top. This will add freshness and a great burst of flavour.

Season with a pinch of salt and freshly ground pepper to taste.

Just eat it

How can you not eat this now while the flavours are fresh and vibrant?

This thing is so healthy and tasty that it's a great way to make non-vegetarian friends, if and when you're ready for that.

Cannellini Bean and Tuna Salad

I love this lunch. It's fast to make, full of flavour, very healthy and it provides you with heaps of energy. Next lunchtime, have a go at making the Cannellini Bean and Tuna Salad with Pickles and Cucumber.

Image: AI refused to follow the instructions. This salad should be mixed together, not served deconstructed, in separate elements like this. Additionally, in AI world, self-evidently, beans are ridiculously huge. Also, I have no idea why the background is a warped, Daliesque version of the Cinque Terre.

Ingredients

1 can (about 15 ounces) Cannellini beans, rinsed and drained
1 can (about 5 ounces) tuna in olive oil, flaked
1/2 cup red onion, finely chopped
1/4 cup pickles, chopped
1/2 cup cucumber, diced
1/4 cup grated Parmesan cheese
A handful of fresh parsley, chopped
3 tablespoons olive oil
Juice of 1 lemon
Salt and freshly ground black pepper, to taste

Putting it together

Mix the Salad Base

1. In a large mixing bowl, combine the rinsed Cannellini beans, flaked tuna (along with its oil for flavour, if desired), small chopped red onion, pickles, and diced cucumber.

Prepare the Dressing

2. In a small bowl or jar, whisk or shake the olive oil and lemon juice until well combined. Season with salt and pepper according to your taste preferences.

Combine and Dress

3. Pour the dressing over the bean and tuna mixture. Toss gently to ensure all ingredients are evenly coated with the dressing.

Add Cheese and Herbs

4. Sprinkle the grated Parmesan cheese and chopped parsley over the salad.
5. Give it another gentle toss to distribute the cheese and herbs throughout the salad.

Eat that Salad

This dish can be served immediately or allowed to chill in the fridge for 30 minutes or more to let the flavours meld together. Just give it a final taste test before devouring it. You may need to adjust the seasoning with more salt, pepper, or lemon juice as needed.

This Cannellini Bean and Tuna Salad is simply great, and the addition of pickles and cucumber adds not only a refreshing crunch but also a very appealing extra flavour profile. Spectacular, just like the Cinque Terre.

FRIED TOFU AND BEETROOT SALAD

Now we head to a little cafe in Tokyo, Japan, where they really want to impress you with a simple dish that is kind to your body and taste buds all at once. Stay with me to learn how you can make the Tofu and Beetroot Salad.

Image: This isn't a bad effort by AI, but the diced, fried tofu should be about half this size.

Ingredients

200g (about 7 oz) firm tofu, cubed and prepared (refer to the previous section on tofu preparation)

1 cup cooked quinoa (cooked according to package instructions)

1 medium fresh beetroot, scrubbed and washed thoroughly in water, and then grated

A small bunch of coriander,, finely chopped

1 inch or so of ginger, grated

Juice of 1 large lemon

3 tablespoons sesame oil

1/2 teaspoon chilli powder (adjust to taste)

3 tablespoons sweet soy sauce

Salt and/or chilli powder to taste

Putting it together

Fry the Tofu

1. Pat the tofu cubes dry with paper towels to remove excess moisture. Heat a pan over medium-high heat and when it's hot on the surface, add sesame oil and fry the tofu cubes until all sides are golden and slightly crispy.
2. Set aside on paper towels to drain any excess oil. Tip: before this, you can first add cornflour coating to the tofu cubes (toss them in a bowl with a little corn flour and seasoning) if you want to add an extra layer of crispness when you fry them.

Prepare the Dressing

3. In a small bowl, mix together the chopped coriander, grated ginger, lemon juice, additional sesame oil (if needed), chilli powder, and sweet soy sauce. Whisk until well combined. Adjust the seasoning with salt or chilli powder as per your taste.

Make the Salad

4. In a large mixing bowl, gently toss the cooked quinoa and grated fresh beetroot.
5. Add the warm, fried tofu cubes to the bowl.

Dress the Salad

6. Drizzle the prepared dressing over the salad ingredients. Toss everything gently to ensure the salad is evenly coated with the dressing.

Eat While it's Hot

7. Transfer the salad to serving plates or bowls. You can garnish with additional chopped coriander or sesame seeds if you like. Enjoy the full depth of its flavours and textures!

This Tofu and Beetroot Salad is awesome and delicious! Just make it.

Salami Skyscraper Sandwich

"Hey Champ! Ya gonna order that sandwich or what? I got a line out the doah! Let's pick up the pace, huh? Come on! We're busy, watcha want? Ya know, the cheddah's aged, but we don't have to! What's it gonna be?!"

Image: This image by AI is more like an engineering feat than food, but it gets the overall New York deli vibe right. I'd slice all the ingredients thinner and use a more crumbly, true vintage Cheddar, rather than a pre-sliced cheese.

Ingredients

2 slices of dark rye bread
2 slices of vintage cheddar cheese
Extra salami (just the way ya like it)
Extra pickles (who don't love pickles?)
Sliced tomato
A handful of lettuce leaves, Chiffonade (thinly sliced)
Mustard - your choice, pal
Salt and freshly ground pepper, to taste

Putting it together

Da Bread

1. It might go without saying bud, but start by laying out the two slices of dark rye bread on a clean cutting board or plate.

Add ya Mustard

2. Spread a thin layer of mustard on one or both slices of bread, depending on your level of crazy.

Layer da Cheese

3. Place the slices of vintage cheddar cheese on one slice of bread, making friends with the mustard.

Add da Salami, ya Punk

4. Layer the sliced salami over the cheese. Then add some more to beef it up.

Pile on da Pickles, Tomato and Lettuce

5. Get them sliced pickles and tomato all over the salami and get that tangy crunch going. Add lettuce on top to freshen it up.

Season it

6. Sprinkle a little salt and freshly ground pepper over the lettuce to make it all pop.

Close da Sandwich

7. Do I need to tell ya? Top with the second slice of bread (yeah, mustard side down, for those in the back row).

Just eat it, buddy why-donchya?

Yeah maybe you can toast it and melt the cheese, but who can wait?

That little New York deli is calling you — just make sure you know what you want before you enter. Then enjoy it with a bit of Frankie Sinatra on the side.

CHAPTER 13
SMOOTH OPERATOR

"SMOOTH SEAS DO NOT MAKE SKILLFUL SAILORS."

ANON

These 10 smoothies are great. They're healthy, easy to make, and can be excellent nutrition before or after a workout or any exercise you might get into. You just need a blender plus whatever is in the list for each one.

Image: If there was a smoothie place, I'd like it to look like this. But what kind of culinary assassin puts a massive slice of watermelon in a glass?

OATS AND YOGURT SMOOTHIE

- Blend rolled oats, natural yoghurt, almond milk, frozen mixed berries, and a touch of honey for a quick breakfast smoothie.

BERRY CHIA SMOOTHIE

- Blend 1 cup frozen mixed berries, one tablespoon chia seeds, 1 cup almond milk, and a drizzle of honey to taste. This one is rich in antioxidants and omega-3 fatty acids.

GREEN TEA AND MINT REFRESHER

- Brew and cool one cup green tea. Blend with a handful of fresh mint leaves, juice of 1 lemon, and a tablespoon of honey. Add crushed ice for extra refreshment.

TROPICAL MANGO AND COCONUT SMOOTHIE

- Blend 1 cup diced mango (fresh or frozen), 1 cup coconut water, a tablespoon of almond paste, and a squeeze of fresh lime juice for a tropical treat. Add a little umbrella on the top if you have one.

STRAWBERRY BANANA BLISS

- Blend up 1 cup of strawberries, one ripe banana, 1 cup almond milk, and a tablespoon of natural yoghurt. Add a dash of cinnamon.

WATERMELON CUCUMBER COOLER

- Blend 2 cups cubed watermelon, ½ cup diced cucumber, 1 cup coconut water, and a handful of mint leaves. This one is perfect for hydration on a hot day, especially after a run.

BLUEBERRY GINGER ZINGER

- Mix 1 cup of blueberries, 1 teaspoon of grated ginger, 1 cup of almond milk, and a tablespoon of maple syrup. Ginger is great for the zesty kick and it helps aid digestion.

CREAMY RICOTTA AND BERRY SMOOTHIE

- Blend ½ cup ricotta cheese, 1 cup frozen mixed berries, 1 cup almond milk and a drizzle of honey for a creamy, protein-rich smoothie. Have this a few hours before your workout.

LEMON CHIA FRESHER

- Combine the juice of 1 lemon, 1 tablespoon chia seeds, 1 cup coconut water, and a teaspoon of honey. Allow chia seeds to swell for 5 minutes or more before blending.

ALMOND BANANA POWER SMOOTHIE

- Puree 1 ripe banana, two tablespoons almond paste, 1 cup almond milk, a dash of nutmeg, and a drizzle of maple syrup for a protein-packed pre-workout drink.

GREEN DETOX SMOOTHIE

- Blend 1 cup spinach, ½ cup celery, ½ cup cucumber, 1 cup green tea (cooled), and a squeeze of lemon juice. The drink you have the next day after the night before. A detoxifying tonic.

Who doesn't love a good smoothie?

CHAPTER 14
WHAT'S FOR DINNER?

"AFTER A GOOD DINNER ONE CAN FORGIVE ANYBODY, EVEN ONE'S OWN RELATIONS."

OSCAR WILDE

As with the other meals, I've designed these 10 recipes to be healthy, relatively quick and easy to make and packed with flavour. Just follow the easy step-by-step instructions and enjoy the experience of cooking your new pasta dishes, stir-fries, simple one-pot meals and more.

LEMON THYME SEASONED CHICKEN WITH SPINACH AND FETA PUREE

Lemon Thyme Seasoned Chicken with Spinach and Danish Feta Puree and Roast Capsicum. That name is a bit of a mouthful, but it's a tasty one! The tang of lemon thyme, the creamy texture of feta and spinach puree, the sweet richness of roast capsicum. Go on and make it tonight!

Image: AI actually did pretty well, here — this image does look pretty close to how I'd serve it, and I love the ambience. It even got the grilled lemon just perfect. But the yellow capsicum (bell pepper) stuffed into a small bowl in the background is super weird.

Ingredients

For the Chicken

4 chicken breasts, boneless and skinless
2 tablespoons olive oil
2 tablespoons fresh lemon thyme, finely chopped
Zest of 1 lemon
Salt and pepper to taste

For the spinach and feta puree

200g fresh spinach leaves
100g Danish feta cheese
1 clove garlic, minced
2 tablespoons olive oil
Salt and pepper to taste

For the roast capsicum

2 red capsicums, halved and seeds removed

1 tablespoon olive oil

Salt to taste

Putting it together

Prep the Chicken

1. Crank your oven up to 200°C (390°F).
2. Season the chicken breasts with lemon zest, lemon thyme, salt, pepper, and olive oil. Ensure they're well coated.

Roast the capsicum

3. Toss the capsicum halves with olive oil and a pinch of salt. Place on a baking tray.
4. Roast in the preheated oven for about 20-25 minutes.
5. Remove from the oven, cool slightly and peel off the skins (or not).

Cook the Chicken

6. While the capsicum is roasting, heat a pan over medium heat. Add the chicken breasts and cook for 5-7 minutes on each side (if they are thick, it will take a bit longer) or until golden brown and cooked through.
7. Remove the pan from the heat and let the chicken rest in it.

Make the Spinach and Feta Puree

8. In a pot, bring water to a boil and blanch the spinach for 1 minute max. Drain it and squeeze out excess water.
9. In a blender, combine the blanched spinach, Danish feta, garlic, olive oil, salt, and pepper. Blend until smooth. Adjust seasoning to taste.

Present your meal

10. Slice the chicken breasts and arrange them on plates.

Spoon a generous amount of spinach and feta puree onto each plate. Add the roasted capsicum to the side.

Carefully pour any liquid from the pan onto your chicken. It's packed with awesome flavour and it's actually illegal to waste it.

Eat it now

Enjoy your meal. You can add a sprig of lemon thyme or lemon wedges to fancy it up even more if you want.

This dish is not only bursting with flavours but also looks quite up itself, making it suitable for impressing any special person you might just want to impress. It's a winner.

LAMB CURRY WITH COCONUT MILK

Want something with a bit of warmth and tenderness? Well before that, try this. It just so happens that this dish includes warm and tender lamb, sautéed with onions, curry powder and chilli delivered with the creamy flavour of coconut and served hot with brown rice and fresh coriander.

Perfect for a cold night or a warm day by the beach in Goa.

Have a go-a yourself. (Sorry, dad joke).

Image: Well done AI, this looks almost exactly right for once. Now can you take me there?

Ingredients

500g (approximately 1 lb) diced lamb
1 tablespoon olive oil
1 large red onion, finely chopped
2 cloves of garlic, minced
1 inch piece of ginger, grated
2 tablespoons curry powder
1 teaspoon chilli powder (adjust according to heat preference)
400ml (approximately 14 oz) can of coconut milk
Salt, to taste
Freshly ground black pepper, to taste
1 cup brown rice
A big handful of fresh coriander, chopped

Putting it together

Prepare the Brown Rice

1. Cook the brown rice according to the package instructions for the absorption method. Once cooked, keep it warm until ready to serve.

Brown the Lamb

2. Heat a large heavy-based pan over medium-high heat.
3. When it's hot on the base surface, add olive oil and follow with the diced lamb. Season with a generous amount of salt and pepper. Brown the lamb pieces on all sides, then remove them from the pan and set aside.

Sauté the Aromatics

4. Using the same pan, reduce the heat to medium. Add the chopped onion and sauté until it's see-through.
5. Add the minced garlic and grated ginger, and cook for another 2 minutes until you can really smell the mix.

Add the Spices

6. Stir in the curry powder and chilli powder, cooking for a minute until the spices are well combined. You may want to add a touch more olive oil if the mix gets a bit dry, and also turn the heat down a touch.

Simmer the Lamb

7. Return the browned lamb pieces to the pan along with any juice. Add the coconut milk and bring the mixture to a simmer.
8. Reduce the heat to low and cover the pan. Let it simmer gently for about 1 to 1.5 hours. Set your timer. You may need to top the dish up with a half glass of water to keep it from getting too thick, so just look at it occasionally and make a call.

Adjust seasoning

9. Taste the curry during the cooking process and once the lamb is tender. Adjust the seasoning with additional salt, pepper, or chilli powder as needed. Throw in half of your chopped coriander once it's cooked.

Serve it up and enjoy

Spoon the cooked brown rice onto plates or bowls. Ladle the lamb curry over the rice and garnish with the rest of your chopped fresh coriander.

Lamb Curry with Coconut Milk is an aromatic and creamy dinner meal that warms you up when you need it. It's hearty, flavourful and healthy for you, especially when you make it with brown rice.

TERIYAKI BEEF AND BROCCOLI STIR-FRY NOODLES

I think you could make this in about 10 minutes. Not even joking. It's that fast. Stir-fry sliced beef and broccoli florets in olive oil, garlic, soy and teriyaki sauce mixed with 2 minute noodles.

Boom!

Image: AI did well with this picture of the dish, but I think it needs to be tossed more, with additional sauce to add moisture. And the broccoli is too large. I'd make the florets (broccoli bits) half as big.

Ingredients

200g (7 oz) thin beef strips
½ head of washed broccoli cut into florets (little pieces)
2 tablespoons coconut oil
2 garlic cloves, minced
1 inch piece of ginger, grated
A handful of basil leaves, roughly torn
1 tablespoon sesame oil
1 tablespoon soy sauce
2 tablespoons of Teriyaki sauce
200g (7 oz) two-minute noodles, cooked according to package instructions
Chilli flakes, to garnish

Putting it together

Prep your Ingredients

1. Ensure the beef strips are thinly sliced to allow quick cooking.
2. Wash the broccoli florets and set aside.

Cook the Noodles

3. Bring a pot of water to a boil and cook the two-minute noodles according to the package instructions. (I'm guessing it says 'two minutes'). Drain and set aside.

Stir-Fry Beef and Broccoli

4. Heat your frying pan over medium-high heat, and then when it's hot, add the coconut oil.
5. Now quickly add the minced garlic and grated ginger to the pan and sauté for about 15 seconds or until you can smell them cooking.
6. Increase the heat to high, add the beef strips, making sure you layer them evenly on the pan so they all cook at approximately the same rate. Let them sit until they start to brown - only about 1 minute.
7. Add the broccoli florets to the pan and move it all around (stir-fry) for another 3 minutes, until the broccoli is tender but still crisp and bright green.

Season the Stir-Fry

8. Reduce the heat to low. Drizzle the sesame oil, soy and teriyaki sauce over the beef and broccoli, tossing well to coat all the ingredients evenly.
9. Add the torn basil leaves to the pan, mixing it up.

Combine with your noodles

10. Add the cooked noodles to the pan with the beef and broccoli. Toss everything together, ensuring the noodles are heated through and thoroughly coated with the sauce and seasonings.

Eat it while it's hot

Quick - get that into a serving bowl. Add some chilli flakes if you like that kind of thing and go for it!

SPICY LENTIL SOUP

This is another simple meal I love, that's great for a cool evening and packed with nutrition and flavour.

Image: I'm seeing a distinct pattern: once again AI made some food thing too large - this time, the lentils. And if you cut your celery that big, you will totally fail the exam. But overall, this is a good effort.

Ingredients

1 cup cooked lentils (either brown, green, or red lentils)
1 large red onion, diced
2 tomatoes, diced
2 stalks of celery, diced
1 cup passata (strained or blended tomatoes)
1 teaspoon curry powder
1/2 teaspoon chilli powder (adjust according to taste)
1/2 teaspoon ginger powder
1 teaspoon ground cumin
1 teaspoon coriander powder
4 cups vegetable stock
1 cup coconut milk
1 packed cup ripped or rough cut, washed kale.
Salt and pepper, to taste
Olive oil for sautéing
Plain yoghurt, for serving

Fresh coriander chopped, for garnish

Putting it together

Sauté the Veggies

1. Heat a large pot over medium heat and add a splash of olive oil.
2. Add the diced onions, celery, and a pinch of salt. Sauté until the onions become translucent and the celery softens (usually takes about 5 minutes).

Add Spices

3. Stir in the curry powder, chilli powder, ginger powder, cumin and coriander powder. Cook for another minute until the spice is hitting you in the face.

Combine with Tomatoes

4. Add the diced tomatoes and passata to the pot. Stir well to combine and cook for about 2-3 minutes until the tomatoes begin to break down.

Add Lentils and Liquid

5. Stir in the cooked lentils and vegetable stock.
6. Bring the mixture to a boil, then reduce the heat and let it simmer for about 20 minutes to allow the flavours to meld together.

Finish with Coconut Milk and Kale

7. Pour in the coconut milk, add the Kale and continue to simmer for another 10 minutes. Season with salt and pepper to taste.

Serve it up

Ladle the soup into bowls. Add a dollop of plain yoghurt to each bowl and garnish with chopped fresh coriander.
Serve hot with Roti bread or crusty baguette and butter.

You'll love the exotic flavour and texture of the Spicy Lentil Soup. And if you don't eat it all at once, it just gets better in the fridge.

Chicken and Pea Risotto

It takes a bold person to walk away from this dish, because Chicken and Pea Risotto is a creamy, comforting dish that virtually everyone loves. And it's easy to make. Do it tonight, and you will find out.

Image: I love this Milanese cafe street scene by AI, but what the heck is going on with the bloody peas? When you make this dish, ensure that you do not have a 1 to 1 ratio of peas to grains of rice. If you remove 50 to 60% of the peas you see here you'll get it right. (And I probably don't need to mention it, but cut the chicken smaller.)

Ingredients

2 tablespoons olive oil
1 tablespoon butter
1 red onion, finely chopped
2 cups Arborio rice
1/2 cup white wine
4 cups warm chicken stock
1 large chicken breast, diced small
1/2 cup frozen peas
1/2 cup grated Parmesan cheese
1/4 cup cream
Fresh chopped parsley, for garnish
Salt and pepper, to taste

Putting it together

Prepare Your Ingredients

1. Heat a large pan over medium heat, then when the base is hot, add the olive oil and butter.
2. Quickly throw in the chopped red onion and sauté until soft for about three minutes.
3. Then add your chicken pieces and brown them a little for another couple of minutes.

Toast the Rice

4. Now add the Arborio rice to the pan, stirring it all with a wooden spoon to coat the grains with the oil and butter. Cook until the edges of the grains start to become translucent, usually about three minutes. You can add a little more oil if it seems a bit dry.

Tip the Wine In

5. Pour in the white wine and stir until it is mainly absorbed by the rice. (Make sure it goes in the dish. Just saying).

Add the Stock

6. Begin adding the warm chicken stock one ladle at a time, stirring very frequently with your wooden spoon to agitate the grains and extract the creaminess of the risotto rice. Wait until each addition is almost fully absorbed before adding the next. Continue this process until the rice is al dente (cooked but slightly firm) which generally takes around 20 minutes. Keep stirring...

Add the Peas (normal amounts)

7. Now stir in the frozen peas. Continue stirring until the peas are warmed through and the chicken is hot.

Finish the Risotto

8. Once you're happy with how it looks and the peas are mixed through, remove the pan from the heat. Stir in the grated Parmesan and cream. Add salt and pepper to taste. You can add some more butter and cream but watch out for the militant health police!

Enjoy this delicious meal

Spoon the risotto into bowls. Garnish with fresh chopped parsley and a little extra Parmesan, if you like. Then get stuck in.

It might be tough to get to Milan tonight, but that should not stop your tastebuds going.

GREEN VEGETABLE AND BLUE CHEESE SOUP

As you can tell by the name, this soup contains green things and blue things, and they're combined in a way that you'll thank me for. It's perfect for a nutritious dinner and is surprisingly easy to make. Here's how.

Image: Even after I asked politely, AI made a lovely green vegetable and blue cheese puree instead. If you make something that looks anything like this, then you've made a great puree too. To make the actual soup, thin it out with more stock.

Ingredients

2 tablespoons olive oil
1 red onion, chopped
2 garlic cloves, minced
2 cups frozen spinach
1 zucchini, chopped
2 stalks celery, chopped
1 head broccoli, chopped
1 potato, peeled and chopped
4 cups vegetable stock (add more at the end if the soup is too thick)
1/2 cup blue cheese, crumbled (castello or any mild blue)
Salt and pepper, to taste
Fresh parsley, chopped, for garnish
Wholegrain bread, toasted, for serving
Butter, for serving

Putting it together

Sauté Onions and Garlic

1. Heat a large pot over medium flame, then add olive oil followed by the onions and garlic, sautéing these until they are soft and translucent (about 5 minutes).

Add the Vegetables

2. Throw in your frozen spinach, zucchini, celery, broccoli, and potato. Stir it all to combine and cook for a few minutes until the vegetables start to soften slightly. You can add the lid on top to make this happen faster.

Pour in the Stock

3. Add the vegetable stock to the pot. Bring the mixture to a boil, then reduce the heat and let it simmer for about 20 to 25 minutes or until all the vegetables are very tender.

Blend the Soup

4. Once the vegetables are cooked, use an immersion (hand-held) blender to blend the soup in the pot until smooth. You can also transfer the soup to a blender in batches if necessary.
5. Return the soup to the pot if you've removed it. If it's too thick, add some more stock and mix through.

Add the Blue Cheese

6. With the soup over low heat, add the bits of blue cheese and stir until it's all melted and mixed thoroughly into the soup. Season with salt and pepper to taste.

Get a Soup Spoon and Go

Ladle the soup into bowls. Garnish each serving with a sprinkle of chopped parsley. Serve the soup hot, with toasted whole grain bread buttered on the side.

This Green Vegetable and Blue Cheese Soup is not only easy to make, but it's also comforting, luxurious, tangy, earthy, sophisticated and very satisfying! What more do you want?

Spaghetti Puttanesca

I love Spaghetti Puttanesca. It's a classic Italian pasta dish full of bold flavours and it comes together quickly, making it a perfect fast, healthy and delicious dinner.

Image: If AI had its way, it would make people choke on black olive pips (seeds) but I don't want you to. So when you make this, ensure you remove the pips first and cut the olives finely. Then you can mix them through the sauce and not die horribly.

Ingredients

400g (14 oz) whole grain spaghetti
2 tablespoons olive oil
1 red onion, finely chopped
2 cloves garlic, minced
4 anchovy fillets, chopped
1/2 cup black olives, pitted and chopped
2 tablespoons capers, drained
1 can (400g/14 oz) canned tomatoes, crushed or diced
Chilli flakes, to taste
Salt and pepper, to taste
Fresh chopped parsley, for garnish
Grated Parmesan cheese, for serving

Putting it together

Cook the Spaghetti

1. Cook the whole grain spaghetti in a large pot of boiling salted water according to package instructions until al dente. 2. Drain and set aside, reserving a cup of pasta water if you need to drop it into the sauce later.

Sauté Onion and Garlic

3. While the pasta cooks, heat the olive oil in a large pan over medium heat.
4. Add the chopped red onion and minced garlic, sautéing until soft and fragrant, which will take you about 2 or 3 minutes.

Add Anchovies, Olives, and Capers

5. Stir in the anchovy fillets, letting them combine into the oil, garlic and onion mix.
6. Add the chopped black olives and capers, cooking for another 2 minutes or so to blend the flavours.

Throw in the Tomatoes

7. Pour in the canned tomatoes and their juice.
8. Season with chilli flakes, salt, and pepper to taste.
9. Simmer the sauce over medium-low heat for about 10 minutes until it thickens slightly.

Combine Pasta and Sauce

10. Add the cooked spaghetti to the sauce, tossing well to coat. If the sauce is too thick, add some reserved pasta water to reach your desired consistency.

Enjoy your Delicious Pasta

Serve the spaghetti puttanesca hot, garnished with fresh chopped parsley and a generous sprinkle of grated Parmesan cheese. (You might also want a little Sangiovese too. Just sayin'.)

How easy is that? Enjoy!

PAN FRIED SALMON FILLET WITH A GREEN AND RED BASE

Pan-Fried Salmon Fillet with a green and red base sounds fancy, but it's pretty quick and easy to make and its healthy. The richness of salmon with fresh vegetables and a zesty balsamic dressing makes a great light dinner.

Image: This is a great vision. Sure, we have an unusual wealth of salt and pepper in the background and no knife, but overall, well done AI.

Ingredients

2 fresh salmon fillets (no bones)
Salt and pepper, to taste
3 tablespoons olive oil
1 bunch asparagus, ends snapped off
2 cups fresh spinach
1 tomato, diced
1 lemon, half sliced and half juiced
2 tablespoons balsamic vinegar
Extra virgin olive oil, for drizzling

Putting it together

Prepare the Salmon

1. Season the salmon fillets with salt and pepper on both sides.

Pan-Fry the Salmon

2. Heat 1 tablespoon of olive oil in a non-stick, heavy-based pan over medium to high heat.
3. Once hot, add the salmon fillets skin-side down. Cook for about 4-5 minutes until the skin is crispy.
4. Flip the salmon over. You might want to add a bit more oil if it seems dry, and cook for another 3 to 4 minutes or until the salmon is cooked to your liking.
5. Remove from the pan and set aside somewhere warm.

Cook the Vegetables

6. In the same pan, add the remaining olive oil, making sure the pan is hot.
7. Add the asparagus, let it sizzle for a few seconds, then add a splash of water or white wine. Cook for about 3 minutes until slightly tender but still crisp and bright green.
8. Add the spinach and diced tomato. Cook until the spinach has wilted, about 1 to 2 minutes.

Present your Dish

Group the cooked vegetables on your plate/s. Place a salmon fillet on top of each vegetable bed. Drizzle the salmon and vegetables with lemon juice, balsamic vinegar and a drizzle of extra virgin olive oil. Garnish with lemon slices and serve immediately.

Sometimes I call this recipe "Traffic Light Fish" since it's red, orange and green all at once.

HALLOUMI AND AVOCADO FAJITAS WITH CHORIZO

This is a fantastic mix of flavours and textures and an excellent example of a fun and healthy dinner. I'll show you how you do it.

Image: Not bad, but once again AI is unhealthily fixated on making the ingredients way too chunky and pristine clean. Make your fajitas messier with smaller bits of everything.

Ingredients

200g (7 oz) halloumi cheese, sliced
100g (3.5 oz) chorizo, sliced
1 avocado, sliced
1 red onion, thinly sliced
1 red capsicum (bell pepper), thinly sliced
4-6 tortilla wraps
2 tablespoons olive oil
1 teaspoon smoked paprika
Juice of 1 lime
Fresh coriander, chopped
Plain yoghurt, for serving
Salt and pepper, to taste

Putting it together

Prepare the Vegetables and Chorizo

Heat one tablespoon of olive oil in a large pan over medium heat.
Add the sliced onion and capsicum, seasoning with smoked paprika, salt, and pepper. Sauté until they all start to soften which is usually about 5 minutes.
Add the sliced chorizo to the pan and cook for another 2-3 minutes, until it starts to crisp and release its oils. Remove the mixture from the pan and set aside.

Cook the Halloumi

In the same pan, add another tablespoon of olive oil and place the slices of halloumi cheese. Fry for about 2 minutes on each side or until golden and crispy. Remove from the pan. Try not to eat them straight away.

Warm the Tortillas

Quickly warm the tortillas in the pan for about 30 seconds on each side, or place them in a microwave for 10 to 15 seconds.

Assemble the Fajitas

On each tortilla, layer the sautéed vegetables and chorizo, a few slices of halloumi, and avocado.
Squeeze lime juice over the fillings and add a dollop of plain yoghurt.
Sprinkle with freshly chopped coriander.

Roll 'em up and eat 'em

Roll up the tortillas and devour the lot immediately. Add extra lime wedges, yoghurt, jalapeños and smoked paprika on the side for added flavours.

These are chewy and crunchy and salty and spicy and creamy and smoky and zesty and healthy. You can't stop after one.

TRAFFIC LIGHT BEEF TACOS

The name is, once again, (like the Salmon dish) inspired by the food colours within the recipe. These tacos are on my menu at least once a week. They're a quick and nutritious dinner option and fun to eat. This recipe combines savoury beef mince with the sweetness of corn and the freshness of tomatoes and avocado. Throw in the right spices and the tang of sour cream and you're done.

Follow on and then you make it.

Image: This AI image of tacos reminds me of every Mexican food advertisement I've ever seen in my life. And why are there so many cactuses? I also have no idea why it decided to use slow-cooked pulled beef rather than beef mince, but we can live with that.

Ingredients

8 soft taco shells
500g (1.1 lbs) lean beef mince
2 cloves garlic, minced
1 tablespoon olive oil
1 can (about 150g or 5 oz) corn, drained
1 fresh tomato, diced
2 tablespoons sweet chilli sauce
1 ripe avocado, mashed
1 small onion, diced
Sour cream, for serving

Fresh coriander (cilantro), chopped, for garnish
1 teaspoon ground cumin
1 teaspoon coriander powder
1 cup shredded cheese (e.g., cheddar or Mexican blend)
1 teaspoon smoked paprika
1/2 teaspoon chilli powder
Salt and pepper, to taste

Putting it together

Cook the Beef

1. Heat the olive oil in a large pan over medium heat. Add the minced garlic and diced onion, sautéing until fragrant and translucent.
2. Add the lean beef mince, breaking it apart with a spoon. Cook until browned.
3. Stir in the ground cumin, coriander powder, smoked paprika and chilli powder, cooking for another two minutes until the spices are well blended through the meat.

Add the Corn and Tomato

4. Mix in the canned corn and diced fresh tomato. Cook for 3 or 4 minutes until the tomatoes are just softened.
5. Stir in the sweet chilli sauce and season with salt and pepper to taste. Remove from heat.

Prepare the Tacos

6. Warm the taco shells - just follow the instructions on the packet.

Make the Tacos

7. Scoop a layer of mashed avocado into each taco shell.
8. Spoon the beef and corn mixture over the avocado.
9. Top with shredded cheese, a dollop of sour cream, and some chopped fresh coriander.

Eat the Tacos. Now.

Eat them immediately before anyone else sees them. If you generously decide to allow any other person near them, they can add toppings like extra sour cream, cheese, jalapeños, tabasco or sweet chilli sauce until everything is gone.

These Traffic Light Beef Tacos are green for go, for any day of the week and any time you want healthiness and fun in combination.

CHAPTER 15
IT'S GETTING HOT IN THE KITCHEN: COOKING FOR YOUR DATE NIGHT

"DINNER IS NOT WHAT YOU DO IN THE EVENING BEFORE SOMETHING ELSE. DINNER IS THE EVENING."

ART BUSHWALD

As mentioned earlier, I was with my ex-wife for 20 years and we were married for 10 of those. Suddenly, being newly single is a bizarre and unusual feeling for anyone, particularly after such a long time together. While it takes time and some getting used to, at some stage in your current journey, you will find yourself looking at dating again. But when is the right time?

After my separation, I was adamant that I was not going to look for any serious partner for years or even consider the idea of marriage again. Of course, I knew there was a world of impressive, gorgeous, brilliant and compelling women online, desperately waiting to hear from me so I could sweep them off their feet and take them to Happily Ever After Land (sarcasm alert), but I was empty and depleted and needed to look after myself. There is no doubt that I was craving intimacy, and the allure of exotic female possibilities was strong, but I was worried that I might just want to be loved by anyone at that point. I mean, I probably would have appreciated slight, contemptuous interest from the Wicked Witch of The West at that point. I knew I wasn't thinking straight, and I could never focus on another person until I focused on myself first.

Inevitably, after about six months of cooking up my new life recipe, I did begin to connect with some women. It was somewhat experimental as I was not expecting much serious to come from it. I just wanted to know if, after being in a relationship for 20 years, I could actually hold my nerve, smile and speak to a woman I liked and make real, sensible, interesting words come out of my mouth, rather than grimacing painfully and providing a horrific jumble of panicked sounds. I'm sure you are familiar with this feeling. The way to avoid that and to make your connections easier is to ensure you are totally comfortable with yourself first and that you are being as authentic and genuine as possible with your new person and everyone else.

Obviously, the potential to find a new partner and go on dates is yet another exciting reason for you to get into shape, eat well and add a little spice to your culinary repertoire. Because once you have got over the (admittedly daunting) hurdle that is the crazy new (for you and me) world of dating, you will begin to see new people and get all the feelings I mentioned earlier that go along with it. And when that happens, and you find a person you like, you'll want to put on a great date night experience.

As I mentioned, there's no need at all to rush any of this, and I think it is a good idea to spend some time making a few of the recipes in this book to get to a level where you are comfortable producing something nice when you're under the pressure of expectation! But once you're at that point, then you will benefit from the experience because you will be able to craft a lunch or home-cooked dinner that you can both thoroughly enjoy. And everyone loves being cooked for.

When I eventually started dating, due to my background in cooking, I was confident in the kitchen so the idea of preparing a special dinner for my date was not something that stressed me out. But I can clearly see how it might make you a little nervous! On that note, I've compiled a few tips that could help you in this area, but the most important thing to remember is that whatever you do, whatever you cook, your date is really going to appreciate it if she's any kind of decent person. Just the fact that you want to take control and make her a meal will win you lots of extra points in her mind. A meal cooked by your date has a lot more meaning than one cooked in a restaurant! Good luck with it all and let me know how you go!

TOP TIPS FOR YOUR DATE NIGHT

Like I said, when you take the plunge and commit to making a home-cooked meal for a new special person, it can feel like a high-pressure situation. But remember how she feels - from her point of view, you're putting yourself on the line (being brave, which is very manly of you!) and showcasing your thoughtfulness, creativity and care. You're trying to make her feel good and comfortable and share a real experience together. That's pretty cool. She has to love the effort, at the very least.

Here's how to ensure a successful date night in the kitchen, even if you're not yet confident with your culinary skills.

What a surprise - start with planning

Make sure you get all the right intel beforehand. That means making sure you've got a good understanding of your date's preferences and dietary restrictions. She will see that you are attentive and that you want to ensure that the meal will be enjoyable for both of you. If you know she loves Italian food, for example, make her a pasta dish. Or, you could get a little inspiration from a movie you've watched together or some kind of shared interest you both have. All these things can make the evening more meaningful. If you want to add another layer of intimacy and fun, you could even do a themed cooking night based on a film or book you both love or a place you'd love to travel together. Do this, and you'll get the five-star rating you're looking for!

Keep it simple

The recipes in this book are designed for learners and situations like a date night. They're not so simple that they're boring but they are straightforward. That's how they are designed and that's fine. Straightforward can also be impressive. It's better to cook a simple dish well, than attempt something overly ambitious, and struggle. If you want to make a meal that's not described in this book just choose something that looks relatively easy to prepare but which will be satisfying for both of you. Ahead of the night, make sure you practise the recipe *at least once* to ensure you're comfortable with the process and can confidently produce a great result.

Preparation is key

Whatever you want to make, do as much prep work as possible ahead of time. That means things like chopping vegetables, measuring ingredients and ensuring you have everything you need before starting to cook. When you get this right, your stress level will greatly reduce and you won't need to scramble while your date is there. You don't want to look like a rabbit in the headlights when you open the front door! The more prepared you are, the more you can focus on enjoying your date's company and come across as the calm and in-control man that you are!

Setting the mood

At the risk of making a massive politically incorrect generalisation, in my experience, women love a little romantic ambiance while they stare lovingly into your eyes. If you don't know what this means, head down to the market and grab some candles, cushions, nice smells, and flowers. Scatter throughout the home. What I'm saying is that the whole vibe of the place is just as important as the food - maybe more important. So before she gets there, clean up the kitchen and dining area, set the table nicely, and get some mood lighting and candles. You can never have too many candles. Soft background music (vital tip: definitely not any sexy stuff yet, and please, please no R&B, and if you even *think about playing Scar* at any time, she'll vomit and leave instantly - don't do that to anyone, ever) can enhance the atmosphere without being distracting. Remember that your date is doing a full-on official international ISO dating standards inspection the whole time, so you'll score very well if you've put effort into making the evening special with nice smells, lighting and music!

Stay relaxed and engaged

Just chill. Remember, the goal is to ensure you both enjoy each other's company. Like any good romantic comedy, there's a strong chance that something won't go as planned. Any other time, it would be hilarious. You might hit yourself in the head with the cupboard door. You might flick spaghetti sauce in her face or choke on the broccoli and go beetroot red before she executes the Heimlich Manoeuvre and saves you. We both desperately hope these things don't happen, but keep a positive attitude whatever fate throws at you. Being able to laugh off small mishaps or near death can be quite endearing. And actually, if you think she'll enjoy it, why not involve your date in the cooking process if they're willing? That could be a fun way to bond and take some pressure off you to provide the slapstick comedy moments alone.

International cuisine night at yours

Whisk her away! Remember that a night at yours can be a night anywhere! Exploring different cuisines can be a fantastic way to make cooking together a more interactive and even educational experience. Whether you're thinking about making something from this book, sushi rolls, a homemade pizza or any other meal, you can choose a dish or travel theme that will spark conversation, interest and fun all at once. You can even pair your meal with a related movie or music from the same country for a fully immersive experience.

Make a seasonal menu

Think like a chef preparing a menu. Look at the season and time of year. You can tailor your menu to the time of year and the freshest and most easily available produce. A light salad and grilled fish might be perfect for summer, while a rich, hearty soup or stew would be ideal in the colder months. Your date will love the link.

Personal touches

What do you know about her? What do you know about her tastes? She is going to know you are a great listener and very thoughtful if you've made a meal that includes her favourite Chardonnay or if you bring out the ridiculously expensive chocolates she raves about after the meal. Incorporating elements you know your date loves, whatever those things might be, adds a personal touch that will put your date night at the top of the international standards ratings, above all others.

Smell good

I grew up with four older sisters, a mum, a step-mum, a step-sister and all their female friends. I've also had two daughters, two step-daughters, an ex-wife and now an almost-wife. If there is one thing I have noticed about women over my life, it is that they are all big on the smells. The good ones. Some dudes, especially those who've been in long term relationships might have forgotten this vital fact. If this is you, don't worry; this is a safe space and there's no judging here. Let he who hasn't sinned throw the first stone, right? All I'm saying is that when she enters your place for the date night meal, you want her to enjoy the aroma of the meal immediately. Just make sure that when you rush up in your chef's apron to hug her and say Hi, your aroma matches the global gold standard she is looking for. It seems obvious, I know, but I'm just putting it out there. While we are on it, make sure you have those nice aromatic candles going, too. Total winner.

It doesn't really matter whether you have a hugely successful meal or you run into culinary issues. We are not competing in Masterchef here. The amount of thought and effort you put into the night will be the thing that impresses your date the most and that she will remember. Cooking for someone is a gesture of kindness and intimacy, and so by planning ahead, staying organised and focusing on dishes that are within your comfort zone, you're going to reveal a lot of positive traits about you and be well on the way to winning her over.

There is a whole world of music to choose from to set the tone and mood on a date night. If you have no idea where to start, here is a sprinkling of musical artist options for you to consider. Just search them up on your preferred music app, play some of their tracks and then let the app keep the mood with its own choices based on these artists (all musical geniuses in my opinion) as the tonal guide:

Angus and Julia Stone

You could choose any album, but I like Down the Way as a starter. It's nostalgic, entirely compelling, very laid back, folksy with a twang, peppered with longing.

Carla Morrison

Déjenme Llorar album; even though she's a Mexican artist, her music whisks you off into a beautiful imaginary place with all the hallmarks of a romantic French movie including the cute red bicycle, decadent cheeses and the clink of two champagne glasses.

Jose Gonzalez

Veneer album; totally chilled, fantastic, quietly reflective guitar and vocals, poetic, like a riverside picnic beneath the final warm rays of an afternoon sunset in the country.

Mazzy Star

So Tonight That I Might See album; enjoy a taste of some sweet, slow bluesy guitar mixed with deliciously seductive, haunting female vocals and effects.

CHAPTER 16
FINAL WORD BEFORE I CLOSE THE KITCHEN

"EVERY NEW BEGINNING COMES FROM SOME OTHER BEGINNING'S END."

SENECA

For me, aside from a few crazy, stressful moments in commercial kitchens, cooking has pretty much always been therapeutic and relaxing for me. If you can get into a routine and enjoy the process, then it is a potential way to find strong ongoing satisfaction. A big part of my message for you and what worked for me, is making your physical and mental well-being a central part of your focus by integrating cooking (the kitchen) and the self-care it represents into your daily life. Do that, plus the exercise routine and some learning along the way, and you will be amazed how good you feel inside and out. It will help you get anywhere you want to go.

Soon after I started dating, I found Susita.

On the first date, we met at the beach and I took my two little girls who were five and nine at the time. Everyone hit it off. I was really surprised at how accepting and happy the girls were about my nice friend. I went out with Susy again, this time without the kids, and met her sister and brother-in-law. We all got along amazingly well and had a great night. We went on a couple more dates that were everything you'd hope for. Meanwhile, I was getting quite confused. I was sure it was too soon to find the right person. And I had already vowed not to get into anything serious and new. I was simply not ready to plunge into a whole other relationship. I told Susista how I felt; luckily for us both, she was incredibly understanding and wise about it. She gave me space as I tried to walk away, thinking to myself that I must be too needy, and it didn't make sense. But it was impossible. I lasted all of three days before I gave in and called her.

We've been together ever since.

Image: This is not an AI cloned version of us, it's the genuine, fully organic, free range, GMO free, artisan crafted, biodynamic couple.

How did I end up with such a perfect match for me so soon after my separation? Luck must be part of it. But more-so, I think it is discipline, planning and focus that powers our luck.

Since we met, Susy and I have barely spent a day apart. When Melbourne was poised to go into Covid lockdown, we decided to stay together at her place. We thought it might be a week or so at home - could be fun!

It was months.

And soon after we were let out, another lockdown was called and it was months again. Susy and I went through the world's longest Covid lockdowns together and got to know each other under that extreme situation. We took it very positively. We were not allowed to go anywhere, so we created new names for the spaces in the home. The kitchen and dining table was the restaurant, obviously. The living room was the cinema. Our bedroom was the hotel. The bathroom was the day spa. The courtyard was the beer garden and the Trampoline was the anti-gravity centre. We worked together from home then, and to this day, we still spend most of the week working from home.

If you can make your ordinary moments special, then everything else is a bonus.

Image: This is the truly horrific 'in captivity' look I accidentally cultivated in lockdown.

When the work day is over we go for kilometres of walks in the nearby bushland and process the day together. We help each other with kids, life and work. Often we will follow our walk with a gym session. When we get home, we throw on the music and cook in the kitchen together. Sometimes the dinner is just the two of us, sometimes it's us and one or two kids and other times it's all five kids and both of us at the dinner table. We keep the music going while we eat. On the weekends, we look forward to spending time together. This is my new family life.

We have our new songs. We've built new traditions in our daily lives, which I have found is really important for both of us to define our new existence. We stay fit and healthy and strong for ourselves and our kids. We never feel like we are working on our relationship, because we are always present in, and enjoying it. We remain grateful that we met and for all that we have now.

Of course we have disagreements. That is totally normal and to be expected since it's only 2024 and still a few years before we fully convert to robots. Even the Dalai Lama struggles telepathically with his Monks occasionally. To deal with any disagreements, we have our processes and communication methods, and as a result, we're able to resolve our issues respectfully. I think the trick is to keep talking and to always be entirely honest and authentic with each other.

Since my separation, I have been a founder of two successful tech business start-ups. I also have my beautiful girls, who I look at as successful human start-ups. They are confident, happy, energetic, kind, grateful, and hopeful little people - successful because of who they are. Maybe we've all learned something on this journey too.

As a person who has suffered the self-inflicted masochistic existence of a tech entrepreneur for many years, at my lowest moment, I was able to bring that entrepreneur's relentless attitude of hope, resilience, opportunity, vision and infuriating positivity to my situation. In the end, my journey revealed critical ingredients to me that comprise a powerful and simple recipe for a new life that anyone can make. And now I'm sharing my story with you to prove it.

The proof is critical.

I'm telling you this so you know the same type of future is waiting for you. Just stay focused and follow the recipe. If you think you're no good at cooking - don't worry. You'll get better. It's the same with dating. Same with exercise. Same with learning. You are becoming a new person, so as with all things, just remember - your persistence is more important than talent!

You'll get there.

I never thought I'd end up separated or divorced, but I did. I had to deal with it when it happened. To do this, I created my own diet and exercise recipe to follow to, firstly, stabilise my life, develop routine and take control, and secondly to rebuild myself physically and emotionally. As a qualified chef with a long-term interest in food nutrition and health, I had the skills to develop a menu that suited this moment in my life, which included a lack of time, money and resources.

I also never thought I'd end up writing a book that might help other men through the same kind of situation I found myself in, but here we are.

Now you can see, almost five years after my separation and divorce, I have navigated my way out of stormy waters to a calm new life of genuine love and happiness. That simple but powerful recipe of a disciplined daily routine, a healthy home-cooked diet and regular exercise has got me here. I am sure you can do that too. Stay on track. Maintain those high-quality inputs. Surround yourself with positive people. Remove the negative ones. Keep persisting in the kitchen. Keep building your confidence in your cooking skills and yourself. Learn new things. Taking control of your situation by taking your own journey through your kitchen and taking care of your body with exercise will provide you with a profound transitional phase in your life that results in a much stronger, more resilient, more capable and happier you.

You will be new.

I'd love to hear about your journey, so reach out to me via my email theofficialchrisgillard@gmail.com with your stories and ideas and to keep exploring and learning in the kitchen and in life. Please view your cooking and all your experiences as an evolving journey you can share with me and others.

I wish you the very best of health and luck for the future. Stay in touch.

> ***"No man can live happily who regards himself alone, who turns everything to his own advantage. Thou must live for another if thou wishest to live for thyself."***

SENECA

GLOSSARY OF COOKING TERMS

These are a few terms you might find in this book and in other places as you hunt for great healthy recipes.

Bake: I don't need to explain this to you but anyway, it's cooking food through the application of dry heat in an oven. Common for roasts but also bread, cakes and pastries.

Baste: To spoon, brush, or pour drippings or liquid over food (often meat) while it cooks to keep it moist and add flavour.

Beat: Rapidly stirring a mixture to make it smooth and add air. This can be done with a whisk, fork or an electric mixer.

Blanch: Before I was a Chef I thought Blanch was one of The Golden Girls, but now I know it's boiling food briefly, then plunging it into cold water. This process is often used to prepare vegetables for freezing, to loosen skins on nuts and fruit, or to brighten their colour.

Blend: Mixing ingredients until they are thoroughly combined and smooth. This can be done manually or with a blender.

Boil: Cooking liquid until bubbles break the surface rapidly. Very scientific. "Boiling" is also used to describe cooking foods in boiling water if you didn't already know that.

Braise: A method of cooking food, especially meat, by searing it at a high temperature, then simmering in a covered pot with a little bit of liquid.

Broil: Cooking food under direct heat in an oven's broiler, leading to a quick char or browning on the surface. With extra time, broil becomes burn, so watch out!

Caramelise: Cooking sugar until it liquefies and becomes a golden to dark brown syrup. It also refers to browning food like onions to develop a richer, sweeter flavour and colour.

Chop: Cutting food into pieces with a knife. Relax, the pieces don't need to be uniform.

Cream: Beating butter with sugar until the mixture is light and fluffy, which is often the first step in making cookies and cakes, followed by licking the spoon.

Dice: Cutting food into small pieces, even little cubes.

Dredge: Coating wet or moist foods with a dry ingredient before cooking to create a crispy outer layer.

Fold: Gently mixing a lighter, airy ingredient (like whipped cream or egg whites) into a heavier mixture, using a spatula in a circular, over-and-under motion to keep the mixture light.

Grate: You already know this is rubbing food against a grater to create fine shreds, right? Great.

Grill: Cooking food on a grill over direct heat, usually from below.

Julienne: Cutting food into thin, matchstick-like strips.

Knead: Working dough with the hands to combine ingredients and develop gluten, which gives bread its texture.

Marinate: Soaking food in a seasoned liquid (marinade) for a period to add flavour and in some cases, tenderise.

Mince: Chopping food into very small, fine pieces. Go slow.

Poach: Cooking food gently in simmering liquid just below boiling point. It's not hunting Elephant tusks. You get shot for that.

Puree: Processing or mashing foods until velvety smooth, often in a blender, food processor or with a masher.

Reduce: Boiling down a liquid to decrease its volume, intensify flavours and thicken the texture.

Roast: Cooking food, usually meat or vegetables, in an oven allowing dry heat to cook it evenly.

Sauté: Cooking food quickly in a small amount of oil over medium-high heat.

Sear: Quickly browning the surface of food at a high temperature to lock in juices.

Simmer: Cooking food gently in liquid just below boiling, with bubbles forming slowly.

Steam: Cooking food over boiling water in a covered pot, allowing steam to cook the food. Not to be confused with 'Steamy' which is hopefully how your date night dinner ended up.

Stew: Cooking food slowly in liquid for a long time until tender.

Whip: Beating food to add air and increase volume, making it light and fluffy.

Zest: Scraping the outer, coloured skin of citrus fruits to use as flavouring, avoiding the bitter white pith beneath.

SOURCES AND RESOURCES

These are a few links to relevant information and support that I thought you might find helpful. It's a bit of further learning, including recommended websites, legal assistance, books and cooking content.

Sallyanne Hartnell - Divorce Coach and Strategist (Australia)

Sallyanne provides support, guidance and care for you, as a person who has travelled the same road. She can help you minimise fallout and impact and redesign your life. This is her site:

Reflectcoaching.com.au

Rachael Sloan - Divorce coach for men (US)

Rachael has a great channel on youtube that gives you fantastic advice about how to approach your new reality as a separated or divorced man. Search this on YouTube:

@RachaelSloanRelationshipCoach

The Family Law Project (Australia)

Shaya Lewis-Dermody started The Family Law Project in 2012 due to frustration about the lack of quality and accessible Family Law services. Since then, Shaya and the firm have won multiple awards for this innovative, impactful and thoughtful specialist family law business. Visit the site:

Familylawproject.com.au

Email: lawyers@familylawproject.com.au

Courtney Ryan

When you are ready for a few expert tips delivered with genuine empathy, kindness and thoughtfulness, Courtney Ryan does dating, fashion and advice for men. Search this on YouTube:

@CourtneyRyan

Nutrition by Kylie

Unlike me, Kylie is an appropriately trained and highly engaging nutritionist and will have a lot more valuable information for you than I ever would. Search this on YouTube:

@NutritionByKylie

Men's Group

This is an excellent approachable, no-stress community and website resource for all men, with groups happening worldwide. They give 'advice for guys from guys' and provide heaps of direct support, self-improvement and motivational training guides. Visit the site:

Mensgroup.com

National Center For Men

This is a men's rights group based in the USA, with over 35 years of experience. Visit the site:

Nationalcenterformen.org

Gaz Oakley

While I am not vegetarian or vegan, I have had periods in my life where I have not eaten meat and I am understanding of, sympathetic to and agree with many of the ideas behind a meat free diet. Whether you eat meat or not, Gaz is a fantastic chef, makes great food and his videos are awesome. Search this on YouTube:

@gazoakleychef

Joe Delaney

Joe is a very relatable dude from the UK who delivers practical workout advice with a dash of humour that doesn't assume you are already a super-cut MMA champion or a Marvel superhero. Search this on YouTube:

@JoeDelaneyy

Chase Hughes

Chase has been called the number one person in the world for behavioural skills and one of the top 40 CEO's in America, under 40. His channel is packed with fascinating insights about human behaviour and neurology that will not only inspire you to be better, it will ignite your passion for more knowledge in the area. Search this on YouTube:

@chasehughesofficial

REFERENCES

To find out more about various bits of information in the book, check out the below.

Mixed Berries

Link, R. (n.d.). *11 Reasons to Eat Berries*. Healthline. Retrieved from https://www.healthline.com/nutrition/11-reasons-to-eat-berries#:~:text=Berries%20are%20a%20great%20source,risk%20(%202%20%2C%203%20).

Extra Virgin Olive Oil

Gunnars, K. (n.d.). *11 Proven Benefits of Olive Oil*. Healthline. Retrieved from https://www.healthline.com/nutrition/11-proven-benefits-of-olive-oil

Avocado Oil

Link, R. (n.d.). *9 Avocado Oil Benefits for Your Health & Beauty*. Healthline. Retrieved from https://www.healthline.com/nutrition/9-avocado-oil-benefits

Physical and Mental Health Links to Diet

Healthy Male. (n.d.). *Diet and mental health in men: Food for mood*. Retrieved from https://www.healthymale.org.au/news/diet-mental-health-men-food-mood

Zelman, K. M. (n.d.). *How to Reduce Stress With Diet*. Everyday Health. Retrieved from https://www.everydayhealth.com/diet-nutrition-pictures/how-to-reduce-stress-with-diet.aspx

Healthdirect. (n.d.). *Exercise and mental health*. Retrieved from https://www.healthdirect.gov.au/exercise-and-mental-health

Health Damage from Ultra-processed Foods

ABC News. (2024, March 1). Junk, ultra-processed food health outcomes study. ABC News. Retrieved from: https://www.abc.net.au/news/2024-03-01/junk-ultra-processed-food-health-outcomes-study/103526352?utm_source=abc_news_app&utm_medium=content_shared&utm_campaign=abc_news_app&utm_content=link

British Medical Journal. (2023). Health outcomes associated with consumption of ultra-processed foods: systematic review and meta-analysis. *BMJ, 384*. https://doi.org/10.1136/bmj-2023-077310

Running for Mental Health

Runner's World. (n.d.). *The mental health benefits of running*. Retrieved from https://www.runnersworld.com/uk/health/mental-health/a39925963/benefits-of-running-mental-health/

The link between Mental Health and Cleaning

Scott, E. (n.d.). *How Mental Health and Cleaning Are Connected*. Verywell Mind. Retrieved from https://www.verywellmind.com/how-mental-health-and-cleaning-are-connected-5097496

The Conversation. (n.d.). *Why is a messy house such an anxiety trigger for me, and what can I do about it?*. Retrieved from https://theconversation.com/why-is-a-messy-house-such-an-anxiety-trigger-for-me-and-what-can-i-do-about-it-211684

Alcohol and Divorce
Divorce Club. (n.d.). *Alcohol and Divorce*. Retrieved from https://www.divorceclub.-com/support/alcohol-and-divorce/

Ria Health. (n.d.). *Drinking After Divorce: How To Handle It*. Retrieved from https://riahealth.com/blog/drinking-after-divorce/

What to Eat for Breakfast
Good Housekeeping. (n.d.). *What to Eat for Breakfast: Start Your Day Right*. Retrieved from https://www.goodhousekeeping.com/health/diet-nutrition/g27684033/what-to-eat-for-breakfast/

The Lobster Thermidor I wanted when I was a kid
Allrecipes. (n.d.). *Lobster Thermidor*. Retrieved from https://www.allrecipes.-com/recipe/87386/lobster-thermidor/

Basic Knife Skills
YouTube. (n.d.). *Basic Knife Skills*. Retrieved from https://www.youtube.com/watch?v=G-Fg7l7G1zw

The Massive Importance of Regular Meals Around the Dinner Table

Berge, J. M., et al. (2014). Family meals. Journal of the Academy of Nutrition and Dietetics, 114(9), 1396-1404.

De Backer, C. J., et al. (2015). Exploring family functioning, ritual meaning, and adolescent outcomes in African-American families. Journal of Family Psychology, 29(2), 236-246.

Eisenberg, M. E., et al. (2004). The role of social connectedness in the well-being of adolescents: Family and friend support. Journal of Youth and Adolescence, 33(5), 315-322.

Fiese, B. H., et al. (2002). Family rituals in the early stages of parenthood. Journal of Marriage and Family, 64(3), 626-637.

Fulkerson, J. A., et al. (2006). Family meals: Perceptions of benefits and challenges among parents of 8- to 10-year-old children. Journal of the American Dietetic Association, 106(4), 526-529.

Hofferth, S. L., & Sandberg, J. F. (2001). How American children spend their time. Journal of Marriage and Family, 63(2), 295-308.

Musick, K., & Meier, A. (2012). Assessing causality and persistence in associations between family dinners and adolescent well-being. Journal of Marriage and Family, 74(3), 476-493.

Neumark-Sztainer, D., et al. (2003). Family meal patterns: Associations with sociodemographic characteristics and improved dietary intake among adolescents. Journal of the American Dietetic Association, 103(3), 317-322.

Rollins, B. Y., et al. (2010). The relationship between family meals and health of infants and toddlers: A review. Early Child Development and Care, 180(1-2), 7-23.

Utter, J., et al. (2018). Family meals and adolescent emotional well-being: Findings from a national study. Journal of Nutrition Education and Behavior, 50(4), 360-367.

Planet Word Museum. "Happiness and Literacy: The Dinner Table Connection." Planet Word Museum, Accessed April 10, 2024, https://planetwordmuseum.org/happiness-and-literacy-the-dinner-table-connection/.

Printed in Dunstable, United Kingdom

68634395R00105